Words We Carry

Words We Carry

Essays of Obsession and Self-Esteem

D.G. KAYE

COPYRIGHT © D.G. KAYE 2014

All rights reserved. No part of this publication may be copied, reproduced, or transmitted in any form electronically, mechanically, or by photocopying, recording, or otherwise, including through information storage and retrieval systems, without written permission from the author. Scanning, uploading, and electronic distribution of this book or the facilitation of such without the author's permission are prohibited. The only exception is the use of brief quotations in printed reviews.

Trade Paperback Release: ISBN 978-0-9920974-6-2
Digitally Published: Mobi: ISBN 978-0-9920974-7-9
Epub: ISBN 978-0-9920974-8-6

DISCLAIMER

Words We Carry is a work of nonfiction. It was written using the author's recollection of events that took place in her life, conveyed from her point of view. The author has changed and omitted some names to maintain the anonymity of those mentioned. The author is neither a medical professional nor a consultant.

DEDICATION

I'd like to dedicate this book to all women who struggle with their self-esteem and to those who have empowered themselves by overcoming their struggles and finding the courage to love themselves.

Acknowledgments

I'd like to thank my friend and fellow author/editor Deborah A. Bowman for generously offering her time and valuable feedback as I prepared to publish this book.

Editor: Talia Leduc
Cover design: Yvonne Less, www.diversepixel.com
Book design: jdsmith-design.com
Ebook formatting: Biddlesebooks

Also written by D.G. Kaye

Conflicted Hearts:
A Daughter's Quest for Solace from Emotional Guilt

Meno-what? A Memoir:
Memorable Moments of Menopause

Editorial Review

"D.G. Kaye offers hope to those of us imprisoned by the negative words and scripts engrained in our minds. Words We Carry, her own true story, tells us how to re-establish our self-esteem and attract the positive relationships we all deserve!"—**Deborah A. Bowman, Author, Publisher, and Advanced Clinical Psychological Hypnotherapist (ACPH)**

Contents

Introduction	1
Why Is Self-Esteem So Important?	5

Section I: Appearance — 9
- The Evolution Of My Self-Esteem — 11
- Vanity—Where Does It Begin? — 17
- Identity And Ridicule — 41

Section II: Relationships — 45
- Alone Versus Lonely — 47
- What's The Attraction? — 51
- Relationships And Self-Worth — 63
- Negativity And Jealousy — 73
- Exposing Our Personality Through The Internet — 97
- Forming Healthier Relationships — 101

Epilogue	105
About The Author	109

"You are the sum total of everything you've ever seen, heard, eaten, smelled, been told, forgot—it's all there. Everything influences each of us, and because of that, I try to make sure that my experiences are positive."—Maya Angelou

"Self-esteem: a confidence and satisfaction in oneself."—*Merriam Webster's Dictionary*

In a state of low self-esteem, we seek the approval of others on our personal quests for achievement. While striving to overcome our perceived inferiorities, we search for ways to better ourselves and compensate for our shortcomings.

Introduction

I wrote this book to share the negative experiences and obstacles I've encountered in my own life. I have tracked my own insecurities and the self-esteem issues of my past in an effort to recognize and conquer the negative image I had of my youth . . . all so I could finally learn to love myself.

Many women suffer from low self-worth. Some may not recognize their existing symptoms, while some may try to disguise their insecurities with self-confident bravado. You may be surprised to learn that many people we perceive as being self-confident share anxieties similar to our own.

Many factors contribute to the complexities we experience throughout our lives, all of which aid in shaping our self-perception. We tend to carry baggage from our wounded egos—from the slights, injustices, and teasing of our pasts—which, when harbored internally, can fester into a damaged soul.

Our habits in life usually evolve from childhood experiences and consequently mold our opinions of ourselves and, sometimes, of others. The fascinations we have as children quite often determine our likes, dislikes, and habits, as well as the personal style choices we make to reflect ourselves through our appearance.

I have been a great critic of myself for most of my life, and I was darned good at it, deflating my own ego without the help of anyone else. I know it began when I was a child. It was then that my obsession with one day being beautiful took hold. My own mother's physical beauty had spurred that desire within me.

With her well-coifed raven-black hair and her catlike emerald eyes, my mother exuded sex appeal. Of course, I was too young at the time to begin to understand what sex appeal was, but from my perspective, she seemed like a movie star, from the way she dressed, to the illusion she portrayed of herself, to the hundreds of times I watched men adore her. I was also too young to realize that the word "beautiful" encompassed so much more than what physical appearance revealed.

When I was a child, my stringy blond hair always seemed to be in knots. My knobby knees didn't do justice to any of the dresses I wore. My face was very plain, with no outstanding features. I was the kid who could easily blend in with the woodwork, with no one to tell me I was cute or pretty. Aside from my nose—which a few family friends told me was "cute as a button"—my looks were very matter of fact.

When I entered my teen years, there were no changes in my appearance other than some weight gain, which didn't help matters. It seemed as though the only thing that grew with me, besides my weight, was my feelings of inadequacy. My mother never seemed to notice my anxieties, never helped me through them, leaving me with only my own determination. I improved myself the only way I knew how.

It took me many years of self-analyzing and experimentation with clothing, makeup, and hairstyles before I reached a place of happiness. I used what I did have, a determined nature and an inquisitive mind, and paid attention to beauty tips from magazines and television in an effort to shake off my inferiority complex instead of drowning in the idea of all I was not.

It was helpful that adults had surrounded me in my younger years, and I had learned to become a good listener, never hesitating to ask questions when I found something particularly attractive about a person or something that person may have been wearing. I was like a junior reporter, taking notes and collecting tips on style and beauty. I tuned in to people's appearances, paying attention to details such as makeup application and trendy styles. Nobody ever knew this about me. I kept my mission to myself.

Fat was something I had neither noticed nor concerned myself with as a child. Only with time and experience did I learn that much about the way we're perceived by others is based on the size we wear. As I matured and endeavored to work on myself, the issue of excess body weight began to plague me. It seemed all my style choices revolved around making me appear slimmer. We can be fat or thin or in between, but the magic of clothing can produce quite an effect, leaving the illusion of a slimmer silhouette when someone wears the appropriate clothing for his or her body type.

We seem to constantly question our appearance by seeking validation of our style choices. Are we accentuating our positive features? Are we concealing what we prefer to hide? Throughout my experimentation with concealing my flaws and conquering my insecurities, I realized that many of our inhibitions stem from our younger lives, which have the propensity to follow us into adulthood. I wanted to tackle my demons rather than fall prey to them.

I discovered that many of my insecurities are rooted in my desire to be socially accepted, to escape from being ridiculed. I needed to find a way to overcome my shortcomings and realize my own worth. To some people, it may have seemed I was becoming vain, but the reality was that this was my effort to look my best, leaving no opening for anyone to make fun of me or call me names the way my childhood peers had. The remembered shouts of "pretty ugly" and "enormous" echoed in my ears even as a young woman.

Words are powerful. They stick with us, never ceasing to remind us how we're perceived, even as children. It's very difficult to disregard those names even after we've found ways to overcome the hurt. I learned, as I got older, that the teasing had followed me, driving me to search for ways to better myself inside and out. Being overweight and awkward had left me an open target for ridicule, and those childhood slights became the measuring stick I used to gauge my self-worth. My experiences as a child had set the tone for my future.

While growing up, I dug deep into my subconscious to figure out what had driven me to do some of the silly things I had done in my quest for self-esteem. As I confronted the origins of my insecurities, preferences, and desires, I also discovered why I had become attracted to certain types of relationships.

And so this book was born.

Why is Self-Esteem so Important?

Women are often caught up in overvaluing the opinions of others, and I don't pretend to be the exception. I've had my share of feeling mocked or judged, most especially in my younger years, when I was still searching for my identity, not yet secure in my own skin.

Ridicule can have long-lasting effects on our psyches, leaving us feeling inadequate or even unworthy of affection. The road toward internal happiness can be long, especially for those of us who've been taunted and teased from a young age.

We need to focus on our positive attributes and stop knocking ourselves down. We don't have to allow others' negative opinions to destroy our self-esteem. It's much more rewarding for us to assess ourselves and, when we find things we aren't content with, use our own power to better ourselves.

If we all look back at our childhoods, we'll undoubtedly remember interactions or incidents that marked the beginnings of our insecurities. We might have been taunted for our looks, our habits, or even for our levels of intelligence. Looking back, we may recognize that the people who bullied and bruised our psyches made those remarks because they themselves were uncompassionate or jealous.

The power of words can lie very heavily on us. The old

saying "Sticks and stones may break my bones, but words will never hurt me" is a fallacy. I suspect that saying may have been first used as a comeback for something hurtful, but the truth is that words linger much longer than physical wounds. The damage done to our delicate egos, especially when we're small, stays with us through the rest of our lives.

We need to overcome these feelings of inadequacy and show the best of ourselves as wonderful human beings. Those of us who despair, letting the mean-spiritedness get to us, obsessing over our personal struggles—be they weight issues, social anxiety, or trouble finding meaningful relationships—need to know that we all deserve to be loved and respected.

Learning to appreciate our great qualities and working hard to overcome the things we don't like about ourselves are giant strides toward happiness. We have to learn to let go of the things we cannot change, recognizing all the positives about ourselves and focusing on them.

Nobody is perfect, we all know that, but when we set impossible goals, we're left feeling like failures when we fall short of our own expectations. It's okay to strive to be the best, but in setting ridiculous goals we only set ourselves up to continuously blame ourselves for the things we are not. Let's not dwell on those things, instead focusing on all the things we are!

Whatever our hang-ups, we need to face and conquer them so they won't eat away at us throughout our lives. If we're unhappy about being overweight, we can find healthy eating plans, ones that allow us to live comfortably and that can be sensibly maintained. If we feel inferior around educated people, we can read books that interest us intellectually or spiritually instead of pining for a university degree. We can allow ourselves to be uplifted and inspired by positive people instead of clinging to negative people who will suck us dry of energy and, in the process, take us down with them.

Above all, we must remember that everything we do to raise ourselves up is for ourselves, because we want to feel good, not because someone told us to do it and not to appease anyone else. This is all about us feeling good and is part of the process of learning to love ourselves. We need to love ourselves before we can truly love and enjoy all other aspects of our lives.

The beauty and contentment we feel on the inside radiate in our physical appearance.

Love thyself.

Section 1: Appearance

The Evolution of my Self-Esteem

When I was a teenager, I wasn't particularly good looking. I was very ordinary and awkward, and I struggled with my weight, carrying about ten to fifteen extra pounds until I reached the age of seventeen, when my weight ballooned by almost fifty pounds.

I wasn't unaware of the escalation on the scale. It had begun as a slow creep, stemming from my having grown up as a nervous child in an unhappy home. My love for chocolate chip cookies had trumped my interest in eating nutritious food. I had grown up with very little parental guidance and certainly no advice about nutrition. My Aunty Sherry was the person who eventually convinced me to join Weight Watchers with her, which was my first introduction to dieting. I was twelve.

Aunty Sherry was my inspiration and my guiding light. My aunt always used to tell me I was beautiful and curvaceous, a pretty word for a girl well endowed with hips. I was petite and very short waisted, and it seemed that although I had a small waist, my calories liked to congregate around my hips. This ratio made my hips an outstanding feature. My weight fluctuated during those years—gain some, lose some—as my momentum rose and fell. My teenage years were the beginnings of my quest to better myself.

I was very aware of my mother's beauty, as was anyone else who encountered her. She was just someone who had that *it* factor that seemed to mesmerize people. As I began to mature, I desired to shed my awkward appearance in an effort to become socially accepted. Family and friends often told me I had inner beauty, but for a struggling teen sitting in school with the beautiful, popular girls, inner beauty didn't quite cut it.

It also didn't help that all of my friends, male and female, commented on how gorgeous my mother was. Some even asked, "What happened to you?" as though I were a consolation prize. I felt the worst rejection when I brought a male friend home after school under the guise of doing homework together, though I was crushing on him secretly. If my mother happened to be home, I could practically see the stars in his eyes whenever he saw her. I felt so deflated and insignificant, thinking I'd never be good enough for anyone. Outer beauty would always prevail.

I paid close attention to the way my mother acted around men, particularly around my male friends. She presented a phoney facade, altering her voice with a hint of sex appeal, which I liked to call her "fake voice." She reveled in moments of praise, and instead of acting like a mom and offering words of encouragement to help erase my insecurities, she left me with feelings of inadequacy while she fed on everyone's attention. It was moments like this that fueled my own desire to be beautiful. I thought if I could be beautiful, people would appreciate me.

I became very aware of fashion trends, at the same time becoming very critical of myself. I hated everything about my body. I wanted to be thin but didn't know how to lose weight and keep it off. I had yet to understand that diets were a temporary solution unless I could learn how to maintain the loss.

I wasn't allowed to wear makeup until I turned sixteen, and I felt that my flaws were constantly exposed. My mother never took me shopping for clothes. When I was younger, she had bought my clothes, but as I approached thirteen, my own shopping addiction began. I had already spent time analyzing my flaws, and I was getting a good grasp on what to wear to conceal my worst attributes.

My insecurity ran wild. My thighs were not small, so I'd buy wide-legged Wrangler jeans, always a size smaller than my actual measurements. My logic was that they would hold me in better, and when I washed them, it was always in cold water, hanging to dry, to keep them from shrinking. I also thought that by buying them smaller, if I got lucky enough to lose a few pounds, they would still fit because I could shrink them in the dryer. Yes, I found logic for every item I purchased. At that time, lumberjack shirts were in. The long, plaid, flannel shirts worn over a T-shirt suited me fine. As long as I could camouflage my weight, everything was good.

At first, my shopping addiction wasn't about buying beautiful, girly clothes. It was about creating a concealing wardrobe. My more frivolous purchases were earrings and shoes, and every Saturday was shopping day for me. I lived for Saturdays. I would go with a girlfriend, taking three buses to Yorkdale Mall, and it was there that I felt in my element—surrounded by stores. That was my happy place, the beginnings of my retail therapy. My dad gave me money every Saturday, but I was never an impulse buyer. I was very methodical about everything I purchased. I had to like it, and it had to serve a purpose, somehow enhancing or camouflaging my worst assets.

I still struggled with insecurity, never completely satisfied with myself. I tried crazy diets from age twelve to eighteen. You name it: the banana diet, Weight Watchers, the grapefruit diet, even the Atkins diet. Most of them made me sick, and my disappointment seemed to lead to more weight gain. I had no concept of how food worked with the human body, being that I knew nothing about nutrition. All I had learned from my aunt was that to lose weight, I had to count calories—and the maximum was one thousand.

When I was seventeen, at my heaviest weight, my dad offered to pay for me to try a new diet called the Dr. Bernstein diet. That diet involved eating about seven hundred to eight hundred calories a day and getting Vitamin B injections to help speed the weight loss. The diet had to be adhered to strictly or one would easily gain the weight back.

After about four and a half months, I had lost fifty pounds! (About fifteen of those pounds were probably unnecessary, as people began telling me I looked anorexic.) Nonetheless, I was tiny. I got a new hairstyle, experimented with makeup, and became acceptably pretty to myself.

My new small self was short lived, though. Nobody had explained diet maintenance to me, and within the next year, I had gained almost all the weight back. At that time, I was about to move out on my own. I had left my tormented childhood behind with lessons learned and many more to come. Luckily, within a year, I had lost all the weight again, and I didn't try any more silly fad diets.

I lived on my own and began to eat properly. I paid heed to my Aunty Sherry's advice about counting calories, and I kept track of what I was eating. I began going out dancing two or three times a week, and I felt good. There were no chocolate chip cookies in my apartment. I became a happier person and found I no longer needed food to comfort me. The weight fell off gradually without my obsessing about it. My eating habits had become a lifestyle instead of a diet. I was very adamant about keeping an eye on the scale, and if I found myself up two or three pounds, a week of being extra strict rectified the situation.

I was still meticulous about my shopping. Everything had to fit just so. You would never catch me wearing a tight waistband, which only seemed to accentuate my hips. My golden rule was to never wear pants with side pockets or pleats—a huge no-no for us gals endowed with hips. Those pants were for the taller, lankier girls.

It wasn't surprising that I wound up selling women's clothing in boutiques for my first few years away from home. I dressed women and developed a flair for style. Although I worked hard on my appearance and achieved many gratifying moments along the way, it still took a few more decades before I could stop being so hard on myself. It was difficult for me to master this because I had grown up so insecure and frustrated, not liking myself, and there had been nobody around to snap me out of my funk and give me some confidence.

Growing up and growing into myself was a long process because even though I had made great progress in my determination to better myself, I didn't notice the changes I had made through the years in the subtle increments of each passing day. I had declared psychological warfare upon myself from a young age without ever realizing how critical I was. The tormented childhood I evolved from had done a lot of residual damage to my self-esteem.

It wasn't until I was twenty that I met my best friend Zan, who pulled me out from the emotional dregs of my inner torment by showing me love and affection. Looking back, I think she saw my inner beauty and looked upon me as some sort of injured bird, buried in a nest, afraid to attempt to fly. Zan saw that I had wings but was just afraid to use them. She never pointed it out to me, nor did she give me flight instruction. Zan was just a beautiful soul the universe had sent to me.

Zan taught me a lot about life. Laughing aloud gradually became effortless for me. I began to have so much to talk about, even the things I had kept buried in my soul—things I had only written about. Zan and I became sister soul mates. She'd hug and kiss me when she knew I needed it, and she also introduced me to the phrase "I love you." She told me she loved me so many times that it eventually instilled in me the confidence that I was worthy of love.

Those were the beginnings of me finding myself and my voice. This was the evolution of me. Through encountering a very dear and deep friendship, I began to learn about life, love, and myself. My friendship with Zan became a journey of self-awareness, and with baby steps, I found new life. Gradually, I grew more confident and happy with the person I was becoming.

Vanity—Where Does it Begin?

I believe that our younger years are when we begin to establish our ideas about what we aspire to become. We're often inspired to emulate the people who influence our lives, but our insecurities can also lead us to make certain choices when it comes to the clothes we wear or the people we form friendships and relationships with. Our fascinations with objects and people can influence the way we choose to present ourselves.

I know working on my physical appearance was a major goal for me because of my feelings of inadequacy. Instead of continuing to feel like a wallflower, hiding in the shadows, afraid to expose my true self and voice, I was going to work on myself to feel more confident. I wanted to break free from the inferiority complex I harbored, always feeling that when people looked at me, they would ridicule or judge me because of my weight. Though my inhibitions may have been imagined, it was frightening for me to want to stand and be counted when I felt as though I had to be perfect to pass the social acceptance test. I had nobody to encourage me.

It was difficult to live with inner turmoil, having nobody to confide in. I made it my business to learn to better myself so that I could avoid spending the rest of my life feeling inadequate. I didn't fully reach the point of accepting a compliment until I was well into my twenties, and that was a process. Not until I met positive influences—and experimented with a barrage of makeup and styling choices!—did I find contentment with who I was and become a happier person.

For many years, I was a fashion experiment. I tried to wear trendy apparel that sometimes wasn't tailored toward my body type. I also tried wearing loose clothes to conceal any lumps or bumps, only to realize that some of those outlandish outfits actually made me look bigger than I was. Then there was the blue eye shadow disaster—you know, that electric blue eye shadow from the eighties. What was I thinking? Zan nagged me about changing the color for almost a year until I gave it up.

Through a lot of trial and error, I began to find an identity, a self I was happy with, and in time, I gradually learned to shed my layers of camouflage and insecurity. I went through a lot of experimentation with clothing and styles in an effort to build my own self-esteem.

Camouflage and Cover-ups

All women have certain perceptions of themselves despite how they're perceived by others. It doesn't seem to matter whether we're size two or twenty: We are good at criticizing attributes we're unhappy about. I am certainly no different. My insecurities keep me constantly on guard about my appearance. My fear of not looking acceptable and leaving openings for ridicule kept me in search of something that would satisfy my desire to feel better about myself. This may seem like vanity to some, but I know my fears of appearing socially inept were the driving force buried in the back of my mind, especially my concerns over my weight issues.

The infamous question asked millions of times by millions of women is "Do I look fat in this?" It comes from a deeply rooted insecurity we all seem to have in us, enhanced by the stigma of society. As a result, women resort to camouflage to conceal our unflattering flaws.

Let's talk about bathing suits, the cause of some of our worst fears. The worst part for me is when I actually set out to buy one. While trying it on in those dreaded fluorescent change rooms, looking in those funhouse mirrors, I cringe. Standing there in my pasty white body, with all my flaws blatantly exposed, cellulite and all magnified, I feel overwhelmed. I struggle to find the best one-piece in a flattering shade. I look for one with the back not cut so low that it exposes any excess skin, one with the legs not cut so high that they emphasize my not-so-slender thighs.

After getting the bathing suit charade over with, I am happily in search of the perfect cover-up to complement my new suit. The cover-up is very important, as it comes part and parcel with the ensemble. It rarely comes off, only when I'm going for a dip or lounging in a chair. I was never going to be one of those brazen women strolling along the beach in solely a bathing suit. This may sound crazy to some, but I don't think I'm alone in this self-conscious thinking. As someone who takes pride in how I put myself together, I do not intend to advertise my flaws to the world. I commend those women who are comfortable in their skin. I often wish I could be like that, but there are just some insecurities I can't get past when it comes to sharing my perceived flaws with the general public.

My shielding tactics extend further than the bathing suit dilemma. I have different methods for different occasions. I used to resist wearing sleeveless tops to avoid exposing my upper arms, a pet peeve of mine—but I touched on that issue in *Meno-What?*, my memoir about menopause, and I can tell you, when your body is bubbling with heat, you learn quickly to surrender the odd insecurity. A dose of hot flashes can really change one's perspective. Perhaps that was what I needed, a good jab of discomfort to help me let go.

We also have those days when we feel bloated—imagined or otherwise. During those times, all we wish to wear are sweatpants and loose tops. I am particularly grateful for the comeback of the tunic top. On the days that I feel sluggish, I can put on a pretty tunic and leggings and I'm good to go. It looks nice and fashionable, and while leggings are expandingly comfortable, tunics are forgiving on those days I feel larger than life.

Many women have issues with their body image, and I can only speak about the things I'm uncomfortable with and explain where I feel my insecurities developed. I truly believe that every individual's insecurities accumulate from prior experiences, stemming from any number of incidents. Name calling, teasing, feelings of inadequacy compared to others, or growing up in an environment filled with discord can all mark the beginnings of our insecurities. Whatever our reasons, they tend to follow us through life, sometimes unknowingly, and these feelings grow into negative character traits.

Some of us go through life denying that we have issues, some reach for help, and others just find a way to hide their damage, living their lives in a shell. I have no qualms about putting my insecurities out there. I've identified my issues, confronted them, and put my best foot forward in an effort to resolve them, to help release myself from them. I've learned to deal with them in a manner that allows me to live happily without dwelling on the negative.

No, I'm not perfect. Nobody is. Even the person who comes off as very secure and confident still has her insecurities, but she may have found a way to rise above them or perhaps to keep them hidden. I'm not making any grand claims about having overcome all of my insecurities, but I can honestly say I've searched deep within to try to understand their origins. I don't pretend to be somebody I'm not, but I also don't feel there's anything wrong with covering up the flaws that make us uncomfortable. As long as I can find a way to feel good about myself, I consider wearing a cover-up or a loose top not as camouflage but as a personal choice to maintain my comfort level.

Our minds are delicate gateways to our egos. Just as a certain song or a waft of a familiar scent may trigger a happy memory, our minds also retain painful memories of ridicule or embarrassment. These unhappy remembered moments are sometimes difficult to let go.

Vanity is a stereotyped perception. When people look great and well put together and come off as confident, they are often perceived as cocky, vain, conceited, or arrogant, though they often struggle with their own issues and have built up their images by overcoming their personal hurdles. I'm not defending arrogance or conceit, merely stating that judgements are often mistaken. Each person, at some point in his or her own life, has battled demons of some sort, so I applaud those who've learned to walk with their heads high.

Not everyone strives to become his or her best self. The world is full of people who wish to avenge their slights and tribulations once they become beautiful or powerful. It is to those people that I believe the word "vain" applies.

A good example of misperceived vanity in my life comes from the time after I left home, leaving behind a dysfunctional childhood, inept parents, and my awkward teenage years. I envisioned one day looking beautiful like my mother, whose outward beauty fascinated me. Inside, however, she had a carefully constructed ego, fueled by her motivation for wealth and attention. She wasn't even aware of her downfalls in so many other categories. She rode the coattails of her beauty in life.

When I was young, I didn't know how delusional my mother was. All I saw was her physical beauty, and it wasn't until my late teens that I noticed how much she used her looks to coast by. When I began analyzing her, I realized there was so much more to being beautiful than our exterior shells. As much as I wanted to look physically appealing, I knew then that I no longer aspired to be like my mother.

Years of experience and friendships allowed me to become the person I wanted to become—a happier, kinder person—and this made me feel so much more complete than just striving for a fancy outside package. Although I became an extrovert, very vocal with my feelings and opinions, inside I was still quite reserved and timid. I found that if I was quiet in a social environment, I was perceived as a snob and was sometimes judged as arrogant. As time passed and I got to know some of the people in my social circle, the first comments I received after truly making their acquaintance were along these lines: "You're such a nice person. I thought you were a snob!" I also heard, "When I first met you, I thought you were so vain because of how you dress. You come off as unapproachable."

These were the first impressions I made.

It's interesting that people can have a perceived notion of someone's character solely based on his or her physical appearance and confidence. I learned that my personality, appearance, and silence in a crowded room had earned me the reputation of a snob. Apparently, I had become intimidating. Learning all this helped me revise myself. I hadn't been aware I was being judged. All that time, people had thought I believed I was really the cat's meow, while at that very same time, I had felt so insecure, wondering if I looked good enough, in an effort not to give anyone the opportunity to make fun of me. While my inner nervousness consumed me, making me awkward and timid, my physical appearance told a different story.

As a person who began to wear her style boldly, I was inwardly shy. Nobody could have figured that out just by looking at me, especially since society only perceives wallflowers as being timid and shy. I, who could stand out in a crowd, was perceived as vain. The personal choice I made to define my style had encouraged people to misjudge my character. I suppose there's an ongoing conflict between the word "vanity" and the actual act of being vain.

We all know that the old adage "Don't judge a book by its cover" refers to more than literature. We all have a past, and our life experiences certainly play a part in forming how we become the people we become. If we can understand and tune in to who we really are and why we acquire our life habits, we all have the ability to make our own adjustments if we really want to.

Have Heels, Will Travel

What is the fascination with shoes? Many women share this passion, yet I'm sure we all have different reasons for becoming obsessed with shoes. I definitely categorize myself as a shoe addict. When people come to my house, the first things they're greeted by are a dozen pairs of shoes at the doorway. As much as I strive to keep my house tidy, lining up my shoes neatly on a mat by the front door, the fact remains that I can never seem to omit the clutter. I find that the most worn or comfortable shoes always seem to be the ones living at my front door until they are swapped around for yet another pair.

I have three closets full of shoes and boots and four more shoe bags, each of which holds a dozen pairs hanging inside the cupboard doors. This may seem like an obsession to most, especially to my husband, but I can justify having so many. (And if I can justify my collection, it can't be that large, after all!) I know where each pair is located. I have them organized by season, occasion, and comfort level, and they all serve a purpose. Does this still constitute an obsession?

Here's the process of starting a collection without even realizing your shoe real estate is increasing. Let's start with basic black. Everyone should have a few black pairs because of their versatility: They go with almost every outfit. We have black boots, black pumps, lower heels, and higher heels for dressy occasions. Then there are sandals . . . and before we know it, the collection has expanded to other styles. The next thing we know, we're expanding our collection for variety, so we repeat the process, adding more colors.

I get overly enthusiastic when I spot a good sale. If I find an irresistible pair and feel it would be sinful to leave them behind at such a ridiculously low price, I don't even think about walking away. I love a good, well-made shoe, and as I age, the comfort level now plays an important part in my purchasing decisions. Of course I own some overly high heels, but if they're purchased as must-haves, they're worn only to events such as dinners, which entail not much more than getting in and out of a car.

I admit to having shoes I can't endure wearing for stand-up evenings, but that's why I have a backup for all occasions. Before I realized it, my collection of shoes had grown enormously over the span of a few years. These days, I prefer to stick to the three-and-a-half-inch heel. I still make exceptions for a must-have shoe if it has a four-inch heel, provided there's at least half an inch of platform on the front to compensate for some of the heel height. So there you have it, a justification for my hefty collection.

I used to wonder if a shoe addiction is something one grows into gradually or if it suddenly sneaks up on us as an obsession. Both options are quite possibly true for some. I'm sure many of us have our own logic for our foot-hugging passions. I know exactly when my obsession with shoes came upon me.

My mother told me that when I was three years old, she took me with her to the hair salon. Women sitting under the dryers sometimes dozed off, and I sneakily took the opportunity to remove their shoes and put them on my feet to strut around in them. Every time my mother caught me in stride, she made me take them off and put them back on the woman to whom they belonged. When I heard about this little ritual, I have to admit I found it quite hilarious. It was also a definite foreboding of things to come.

My first recollection of my love for shoes goes back to when I was four and my dad took me to my uncle's shoe store to buy me a pair of black patent party shoes, complete with bows and a tiny heel. I loved those shoes because they weren't school shoes or play shoes, they were the real deal. I wore those shoes inside the house as much as I could, because wearing them only for a special occasion wasn't enough. I was told to take them off many times after getting caught clacking around in them on the hardwood floors. I remember the sadness I felt when my feet began to grow out of those shoes. I was finding it near impossible to squeeze my little toes into them any longer.

    I don't recall owning another pair quite like them until I was well into my teens. The only things that brought me as much excitement as having those party shoes as a child were the red plastic high heels with silver elasticized straps that my mother brought back for me from one of her pleasure jaunts to New York City. I was six, and I thought I'd died and gone to heaven, having my own high heels, as I clicked away with every step I took. I never wanted to wear any other shoes again. I wished I could wear those plastic shoes anywhere and everywhere. I shed so many tears over them when my mother shot down my constant begging to wear them all the time.

    Eventually, as I got older and those red shoes no longer fit me, they were thrown in the garbage, but my yearning for heels never subsided. When my mother wasn't home, I had a feast in her closet, trying on and wearing her pointy-toed high heels around the house while playing dress-up.

    On the weekends I stayed at my grandparents' home, I suffered immensely from shoe withdrawal, because my grandmother was very old fashioned and only wore "grandmother shoes," as I called them. They were black and orthopedic looking, in a sense, although they did have a wide two-inch heel. They reminded me of the type of shoes nuns wore back in the sixties and seventies. The only thing that excited me about those shoes was the sound they made when my grandmother would take my siblings and me out for a walk on Saturday afternoons.

The route we took was paved with cobblestones. I loved the satisfying sound her heels made as they clicked on the ground with her every step. Other than those shoes, which my grandmother wore all the time, I discovered a pair of turquoise blue satin pumps in a shoebox she had stowed away in the back of the linen closet, on a high shelf. If I hadn't been such a snoop, I would never have known about those gems. When I told her I had found them, she allowed me to clomp around in them at her house, which only fed my desire to wear high heels.

A few years later, the only affection I've ever felt for a flatter shoe came when my mother's friend took her laundry to the dry cleaner. This dry cleaner used to run promotions for years, and if you spent a certain amount, you could earn a pair of Chinese slippers of your choice. Nowadays we may recognize them in our local dollar stores made of basic plastic, and they come in an array of colors with little beads on them. Back when I was a kid, though, those slippers were beautifully made of satin, and embroidered on them were vibrantly colored patterns.

My mom's friend was childless and knew of my fetish for shoes, and whenever she accrued enough points to receive a pair, she always got them for me. I eagerly anticipated each new pair. Whenever she came to my house, I got so excited, hoping she had another pair for me. After that phase, it was onward to the high heels that could give me a thrill.

By the time I turned thirteen, my feet had stopped growing, and I was delighted to find that my mother's shoes fit me perfectly. My mother's frequent absence left me in shoe heaven, with the opportunity to wear her shoes to school. By age fifteen, I was beginning to accumulate my own private stock of quite an assortment of heels. I had finally graduated to having my personal love for shoes fulfilled by buying the shoes I loved all for myself. It was a great bonus for me that my feet remained at size six—the perfect sample size!

How coincidental was it that a girl obsessed with shoes would wind up with the most convenient shoe size? This size affords me the luxury of walking into any shoe store and trying on shoes endlessly without ever having to wait for assistance from a salesperson. Only when I've made my decision do I have to ask someone to bring me the pair I've chosen to purchase.

When I ask myself if shoe obsession is an acquired art, I would have to answer that for me, it was certainly something that grew with me from childhood. To all my friends out there who constantly ask me how I can have so many shoes, you now know how it happened.

The world is full of shoe-lovers. For some it begins as a fascination, and for others it may be just the thrill of acquiring a collection. It's funny how everyday objects can become treasured obsessions.

I still can't say for certain what fueled my childhood obsession with shoes. I suppose it was part of my fascination of beautiful things. When I observed women strutting by in their high heels, I was captivated by the eloquence of their expression, how they emphasized the swish of a flared skirt with every clacking step. Something about the clicking sound of the heels as they hit the pavement was very intriguing to me.

As I grew older and began my quest for self-acceptance, I realized that pretty shoes with high heels were not only something to admire, they also served a great purpose. They added height, and somewhere in my deductions, I had equated height with looking thinner. As I was obsessed with my weight through my younger years, my high-heeled friends became a staple in my wardrobe. Thank you for sharing the love, Carrie Bradshaw!

The Bigger the Hair?

I love big hair, the bigger the better. For some of us, creating a big hairdo is an art. I've had this theory since I was a teen: The bigger my hair, the more slender my frame appears.

Back in the day, there weren't nearly as many hair products available as there are now. So many hairstyles have evolved through time, and now the shelves abound with a plethora of choices. In my younger days, I was sure that I was one of the forgotten ones, having been gifted with long, straight, flat hair that matted around my face and didn't do my chunky frame any justice.

It didn't seem to matter what tactics I tried. I curled my hair to add body. I used hot rollers—electric and steamed in a pot—and scratchy bristled rollers overnight. The results were the same: Within an hour, my hair was back to its stick-straight preference, refusing to hold a curl.

By the time I turned eighteen, in my quest for big hair, I had become a big fan of the "permanent." By that time, the chemically highlighted blond streaks on my already blond hair, with the addition of perming chemicals, had left me with a shredded wheat-like effect. My mane didn't feel particularly luxurious to the touch, but the residual damage from all those processes seemed to thicken the volume of my hair because of the damaged hair cuticles. The result? I had volume, and lots of it. Who would have thought that all that chemical damage would thicken my hair? I loved it!

The crazy things I did in the name of vanity, without any regard for the abuse I put my hair through, make me shake my head now—another reminder of how oblivious we are to the future when we're young. The joy of being carefree, with no regard for tomorrow, is an innocence we sometimes long for when we grow older.

Hairstyles change all the time. Some were silly fads, and some involved a lot of work. Many styles have even made comebacks. With different styles, there are always new products advertised, but the basics never change. One needs a good teasing comb, a blow dryer, a good thickening product, and the ever-popular hairspray if one is going to fight the battle for volume.

I've lost count of how many sets of rollers, curling irons, and styling brushes I've had over the decades. Hair and fashion styles change with the years, but if you live through enough of them, they all seem to come back, reinvented. Our hair is our crowning glory, no matter how much or how little we have of it.

Some of the names given to hairstyles make me laugh, and many of them are self-explanatory. Take the beehive, for example. What a fitting name! Hair piled up on the head, looking ample enough for a swarm of bees to hide out in. That style was popular when I was about three years old, and it's not one I'm really interested in seeing make a comeback. I also had a terrifying dislike for the pixie cut, which, admittedly, I was a victim of once in my childhood. I was mortified and cried for weeks when my mother decided that it would be a cute look for me. Although I was around seven at the time, I already knew I would never allow myself to be without longer locks again, and, consequently, I haven't cut my hair short since that fashion disaster.

In my teens, the popular look was the Farah Fawcett haircut. That shaggy, wind-blown look was so alluring to me. It was a style I aspired to wear, but, sadly, my hair texture didn't want to comply.

Men have their own issues to deal with. With the onslaught of male pattern baldness as they age, many of them will use whatever they have left to create the illusion of more hair. One memorable style that comes to mind is the comb-over. You know that method men use when their hairlines begin to recede and they sweep strands from one side to the other to try to conceal the bald spots on the tops of their heads?

Throughout time, we are obsessed with our hair. We want to keep up with current styles, but we have to be cautious about what looks suit us and to what styles our hair is actually capable of adapting. The beginnings of thinning and graying are certainly blows to our egos, but that's human nature.

When I was a young schoolgirl, it seemed that all the girls like me, with straight hair, craved curls. What I found puzzling was that the girls with curls often complained that they couldn't tame their locks and wished for straight hair. I couldn't even begin to understand that. With the countless times I spent at the beauty salon, streaking and perming my hair, I was surprised to see other women having chemicals put in their hair to relax their curls and waves.

When I turned forty, the phrase "Be careful what you wish for" became my reality. I was stunned to find out how much our hormones dictate our hair texture. I became ill at the time and was prescribed steroids for several months. With all the turmoil I endured with my illness, I miraculously discovered that my lifelong straight hair had suddenly become wavy. To this day, over a decade later, my hair remains wavy. I was mystified by this happy side effect. That's the power of drugs that disrupt the hormonal system!

I never imagined that my woes, all those hours spent trying to get a curl to hold, could be remedied by steroids. I had to become very ill before nature reversed the curse of my straight hair and gave me curls in compensation. I had joined the league of women who had issues with frizzy hair in humid weather, but it honestly didn't bother me as much as it seemed to bother other women. After all, it left me with big hair, and that was all I had ever wanted in the first place.

Over the years, I've still used my trusted hot rollers for added lift at the crown of my head. I changed my once blond hair to red decades ago, and my hair products seem to be taking over my bathroom. I went through a phase of thinning hair during menopause, but my determination for big hair prevailed. After my hormones stopped being at war with each other, my hair stopped misbehaving. In my search for improved hair products to regrow and reinforce my strands, I remain true to my big hair.

Making My Mark with Orange Lips

One of a woman's most coveted beauty aids is lipstick. A question often posed to women is "If you could only keep one of your most favorite makeup items, which would it be?" The answer is always lipstick, with mascara coming in at a close second.

What is the fascination with lipstick? It has the ability to perk up and brighten one's whole face. Even in the absence of any other makeup, lipstick can lift our appearance and spirits. It keeps us from feeling naked and exposed, and it can help redefine the shape of our lips. Aside from the plethora of colors available, there are also a myriad of scented and flavored lipsticks and glosses. I honestly can't recall any moments when my lips haven't been covered by either lipstick (when I go out) or some sort of lip balm or clear gloss (when I'm home or getting ready for bed, just to keep my lips moist). I'm definitely a lipstick girl, though I no longer care for glosses because of the feathering they seem to create around my lips.

I can recall my strict mother forbidding me from wearing any makeup before I turned sixteen. After much coaxing on my part, she finally allowed me to wear lip gloss when I turned fourteen. That was a big thrill for me because I could finally wear something to improve my looks, using color to bolster my self-esteem. I remember the thrill I had when going to the drugstore, being able to choose a color on my own.

I was no different from the average girl when experimenting with lip gloss. It was all so fascinating. The array of colors to choose from left me feeling euphoric. Glosses with wands and dipping pots, chocolate and fruit flavors, and scents of peppermint and cinnamon lined the shelves, all having their own distinctive alluring appeal. The more colors I collected, the more fun it became to experiment and find which felt or tasted the best or which lasted longest. I sometimes had no regard for whether the color even suited me. The fun was all about acquiring colors, with enough varieties to match anything I wore.

As we get older, we advance to the more high-end lip products and begin expanding our tastes to brand and designer lipsticks. We discover liners and serums along the way. The appeal of an exciting lip gloss grows into a serious art of lining, mixing, and blending colors to attain the perfect pout. Sometimes we choose a color to match an outfit, sometimes just because it's a trending color. Eventually, through the years, most women decide on a shade they're comfortable with, and some may adopt a color as their own signature.

After a long time of searching for the perfect color and going through some poor choices along the way, wearing trendy colors that did nothing to complement my skin tone, I finally found my lipstick happiness. Through a process of trial and error, and being a fan of rich pigmented color, I was hooked on fuchsia lipstick while in my blond days. It was the perfect addition to my colorful new personality.

When I became a redhead, I quickly learned that fuchsia clashed with my new shade. I went through the experimentation process again, wearing shades of mocha and light brown, but I wasn't happy with the conservative look those shades reflected. As I grew older, I became much more extroverted, and I needed a shade that would satisfy my lust for color. At last I found it: orange.

I crept into the orange phase slowly. I felt one had to ease into such a bold color gracefully so as not to give off a clown effect. I began with variations on orange, more rusty at first, and gradually worked my way into burnt oranges until I finally fell in love with bright coral. When I reached a satisfactory confidence level within myself, I became very comfortable wearing this sunny color. It complemented my skin tone and hair, and it faithfully became my signature color.

I will say that when I began wearing orange lipstick, well over fifteen years ago, it was a difficult color to obtain—not popular, and difficult for many women to wear effectively. Through the years, my exact shade of orange varied as cosmetic companies came out with newer, albeit limited, selections. I also learned the word "discontinued" very well as time passed.

Experience taught me that if I loved a color, I needed to stock up on it. It seemed the orange shades were often discontinued because of a lack of sales. I couldn't pass a makeup counter without checking whether there was something new in my favorite color. People who knew me were so used to seeing me with my signature orange lips that if I strayed to a different color, not as vibrant, they would comment.

I couldn't fathom how so many women couldn't covet the color as I did. When I thought about it, though, I never really noticed anyone wearing my colors. I supposed the statistics were accurate, and I realized I was in a minority. It didn't bother me or intimidate me. I felt good about myself after spending years building my self-esteem. Some saw me as bold for wearing such a bright lipstick. Cosmeticians often complimented me for the vibrant shade I sported while passing their counters.

Ironically, only in the past two years has orange lipstick gained popularity, becoming a fashionable color. Imagine that, I was finally in style! Upon reading that orange was in, I giggled to myself with a sun-kissed smile.

Many women are intimidated by color, as I remember once being. During my years of low self-esteem, the last thing I would have wanted to do was draw attention to myself by wearing bold colors. I did long to wear vibrant shades, though, because bright colors made me feel happy.

As I matured and became more confident in myself, I developed my own personal style, and bright lipstick was definitely part of that ensemble. Wearing bright lipstick wasn't about seeking attention—it made me feel empowered and was an expression of my personality. I had worked hard to break out of my introversion. The colors I began wearing projected my confidence. I was no longer afraid to be who I wanted to be. I was ready to be me, and if that meant some would stare at me for my vibrancy, I was ready to stand up for myself.

I grew into my big personality and became less timid as time passed. Instead of feeling insecure when people stared at me, I learned to smile. Sometimes looking someone in the eye and smiling can intimidate them, making it difficult for them to judge.

After the shock of orange lips wore off on people, they came to expect it, and they'd wonder whether something was wrong if I dared stray to another color. This is how you know you've established your brand.

We have to be bold to let people know how we wish to be recognized. We shouldn't be hindered by our insecurities when we wish to express ourselves. We're all entitled to choose how we wish to express our identities—for ourselves, not for others. We have to accept that we're never going to please the whole world, so why not please ourselves?

Wearing Makeup

Are we considered vain because we wear makeup? Does doing so signify insecurity, or does makeup help identify us? Perhaps, for me, it's a little of each. All women have their own reasons for wanting to wear makeup. Some do it to enhance their features, and some do it to camouflage themselves. Makeup is an expression of ourselves.

Numerous products encourage us to express ourselves through our makeup. We can change our features by lifting our cheeks with a stroke of blush or perking up a droopy eye with an upticked wing of eyeliner. If we line our lips slightly outside of our natural lip lines and fill them in with matching lipstick, voila! We have thicker, fuller lips.

Yes, I've learned all the little tricks through years of trial and error while searching to make the most of my looks. Some people are skilled at the art of makeup application, and others prefer to cake it on, believing more is better. Whatever our reasons or methods, wearing makeup just makes many of us feel better about ourselves. That's the bottom line for many of us gals.

As a teen, I couldn't wait to wear makeup to help transform my "blah" looks into something more refined. It took some years before I developed a look that I felt comfortable wearing, one that still left me looking like me. My need to look good and feel good about myself drove me to embrace so many fads, but deep inside, it was always my inferiority complex that drove my obsession. Once I began wearing makeup, I *never* went anywhere without it.

No, sir, I wasn't going to be caught off guard anywhere without my face on. One never knew whom they might unexpectedly encounter. I was always prepared. That was the way it began for me, and that's the way it still is. I was so obsessed with never being caught without my face on that I was tormented by one question for years while I was single: How could I avoid letting my husband see me without makeup once I got married? That's obsession! I have to believe I wasn't alone in that line of thinking, though. Our quest for beauty can sometimes lead us to think some pretty strange thoughts.

My worries about staying hidden in my makeup seemed to dissipate as I grew older. I began to realize that there was more to myself than just looks, but that all took time to learn. It took a long time for me to be happy with and to love myself. I shudder at some of my crazy logic back in the days.

My newer thinking told me that if a guy didn't like what he saw without makeup, well, guess what? He wasn't worthy of me. Okay, this didn't mean I began going out without makeup on. It meant that I learned how to feel comfortable in my own skin, in my own home. It took a lot of discipline for me to learn that every time I had a visitor drop by or even if I was just going across the street to fetch my mail, it wasn't necessary for me to wear makeup.

Some people do look very different without makeup. I realized, though, that because I had taken good care of my skin, I really didn't look as scary as I thought I did. I was just a plainer version of myself, and I sometimes found that I looked younger without my glam face, though it took me decades to recognize this and admit it to myself.

I recall an experience in my twenties with an old boyfriend when I slept over at his house for the first time. I wasn't very good at being spontaneous. Sleeping out was something I had rarely done because I always had to have my arsenal of beauty weapons handy. I hated sleeping in makeup, and I was worried about him seeing me for the first time without any.

The next morning when I awoke, I found him perched on one elbow with his hand supporting his head. I could feel him peering at me while waiting for me to awaken. I opened my eyes slowly, and I immediately threw my hands up to my face to cover it. I was begging him not to look at me. He laughed and rolled over and hugged me. He told me I was beautiful. I cringed because I couldn't accept it, as much as his compliment had given me a glimmer of hope that maybe I wasn't such an ugly duckling without my makeup on.

Makeup was like a protector for me in the outside world. It didn't define me, yet it padded my sense of security. It was like wearing a shield that hid my plainness. As much as I had become more accepting of myself, I knew I had a tendency to keep my little hang-ups buried inside, no matter how much therapy I gave myself. I seemed to be a work in progress, but that was the key—to keep working so that I could one day accept myself.

I think it serves us well to remain humble when we remember how much angst we suffered when we were younger in order to fit in. A little bit of humble pie reminds us of just how far we've come without allowing the new and improved versions of ourselves to inflate our egos.

I'm much more confident now after years of self-analysis, but don't be mistaken: I still have days, as many do, when I dislike something about myself. Perhaps it may be a bad hair day, or I may be retaining too much water, but I've learned to deal with it. I just put on a hat or a headband, slip on a pair of leggings and a roomier top—and of course I put on my makeup, bright lipstick, and I always wear my smile!

Weighing In on Life

The scale is a big obsession for many women, one that I harbor, as well. The scale is the enemy. It is not our friend. It's meant to keep our weight in check, but for me it has become a means to measure my worth. Growing up chunky helped fuel my fear of the scale.

Many people dread going to a doctor's appointment because of the fear that they'll be ordered onto the scale. In my heavier days, I wasn't remotely interested in seeing the number on the scale, and I certainly didn't want anybody else, particularly a doctor, recording it. It wasn't until I got my weight under control that I became happier about myself and stopped being so concerned with the scale. The fear of the fifty pounds I had gained as an unhappy teen was enough to keep me on track if I ever slipped.

My weight stayed pretty much the same for decades, bouncing up or down by five pounds. I suffered two hefty setbacks throughout the years with two major illnesses. The first was Crohn's disease, for which I was put on steroids, and I magically gained twenty pounds within three weeks. The second time occurred after I had open-heart surgery, when I was in the hospital for five days. When I went in, they weighed me, and I was around 128 pounds. In those five days, I barely ate—yet I came home weighing 152 pounds! I was so weak and found it difficult to breathe, and I felt that something wasn't quite right. My sister took me back to the hospital the day after I returned home, and the surgeon told me that for some reason, they had failed to give me water pills to release the amount of saline pumped into me during surgery.

I went home with my new "pee pills," and I miraculously lost twenty-four pounds in three days! Ah, yes, if only life were like that. That obviously wasn't weight gain but rather *huge* water retention. It wasn't any wonder I felt like the Goodyear Blimp. That was a lot of pee! Other than those two incidents, though, the scale wasn't a big issue.

Enter the menopause dragons.

They were a completely different animal. Gradually, my patterns of eating well and doing moderate exercise became no match for my mixed-up hormones, which had chosen the parts of me that they wanted to make their home. Muffin tops and bloating became permanent visitors. Oh, yes, we read about it, hear about it, and still we think it's not going to happen to us. Many women do encounter the dreaded middle-aged spread. I took it as an assault on all the hard work and discipline I had put into my weight management over the years, and it made me crazy. Imagine not straying from your diet and health plans only to find them slapping you in the face when your body starts doing weird things!

My choice of wardrobe was dependant on the extent that my stomach stuck out on any given day. It wasn't as bad during perimenopause as it was post menopause, when the dust settled. Once again, the past had come back to haunt me. I was fighting the battle of the bulge.

I began trying everything to lose my newly acquired spare tire. Thankfully, the scale registered only a five-pound gain, but five pounds around one area felt like twenty. My scale obsession was reignited with every new diet and exercise I tried. I couldn't get over the fact that everything I did to try to lose weight wasn't working.

I started moving that scale around to different rooms and different spots on the floor. It seemed that every time I moved the scale, the number would read a pound heavier or lighter. I had to see a better number! After months of playing that game, it got to the point where I didn't even know what the real number was. Sometimes I'd go pee and hurry back on the scale in hopes that I may have lost half a pound just from water loss. Heck, I even tried exhaling hard and jumping back on to see if the amount of air in me would alter the number.

Many times, I kicked my scale in frustration. Sometimes it left a ding in the baseboard. I lost count of how many times my husband asked me why the scale was sitting in an awkward spot on the bathroom floor after I had kicked it in my angry state. Yes, I was completely obsessed.

My husband heard all my complaints about my new self, and he'd laugh each time I went off on a tangent about my fat. To this day, he assures me I'm not fat. I honestly don't know if he doesn't notice my fuller waistline or if he chooses not to admit he notices. It's reached a point with me where I don't complain anymore, and I'm grateful that he always compliments me and chastises me for being so hard on myself.

I am blessed to have such an adoring husband, but I have to say that it doesn't resolve my unhappiness about my newer zaftig look. Life really is a circle. We sometimes think we've battered our demons for good only to have them resurface at another point in our lives. I refuse to give up the fight. I am adamant in fighting my war on fat instead of surrendering to it.

I've spent over a year, now, battling that little demon. I've decided I'm not going to starve myself or work out like a maniac to further aggravate my sluggish metabolism, but I've tweaked my wardrobe like I did in my younger days, dressing with style without accentuating my weaker features. Through all my efforts, I haven't gained any additional weight. Slowly, as the days and weeks go by, I'm trying to adjust to the new way my body chooses to be. I'm slowly losing my anger over it and trying to be accepting of it as a part of what my body has gone through.

I'm still learning to avoid being my own worst critic, but it's an ongoing process. At least I'm always trying. I know the alternative. If I throw my hands up in defeat and let myself go, it would only lead me to a much unhappier place. So I choose to remain positive, tuck one more feather of achievement in my cap, and embrace my life.

Identity and Ridicule

Searching within ourselves in an effort to discover our own identities begins when we're young. We follow the examples of those who influence our lives, such as family and friends. Eventually, as we mature and our curiosities awaken, we begin to recognize how our personalities are developing. We formulate personal opinions and goals, which play an integral part in who we become. The influences around us usually determine the habits into which we tend to fall.

We pick up bad habits or inferiority complexes from our home environments or, later, from the friendships and other environments we choose. We eventually adapt to our habits, and as we age, either we take with us the negative baggage we've acquired since childhood or we become aware of it and endeavor to find resolution and better ourselves. The latter isn't always so easy to accomplish. The lucky few who learn to overcome their inner struggles live peacefully within themselves, in time.

Many people seek professional help to conquer their identity issues. Others may not be able to get past prior hurts and slights and continue through life carrying the weight of inadequacy. It's often more difficult to accept ourselves if we have no positive parental influence to guide us through childhood with nurturing and encouragement.

We all have the freedom to become what we want to be and

to affect the way we're perceived by others, but some people don't use this power. Whether they realize it or not, they get caught up in the realm of merely existing based on what they were taught.

Identity is a brand that signifies who we are and what we stand for. Our beliefs and values signal what kinds of people we are. Our outside trappings—our physical appearance and mannerisms—reflect how we project ourselves and how others perceive us.

The struggle to find our identities is particularly delicate in our younger years—the high-school years. These are the years we begin comparing ourselves with our schoolmates. We begin to notice the popular girls, the pretty girls, the girls who attract male attention. For many of us, this is when admirations, jealousies, and feelings of inadequacy begin to take root. We want to be like those popular girls, and perhaps we want to acquire a style of our own, to reflect our own unique brands.

Some feel threatened when competitiveness strikes, feeling that their self-worth declines because they're not popular. Those crushing feelings linger, becoming inadequacy. This happens particularly when we don't have positive influences in our lives to encourage us and lift our self-doubts. Even worse, girls are often teased and bullied purely because of their physical attributes, because they don't fit with what society dictates as socially acceptable. Without proper attention, bullying can be detrimental to a person's life and can contribute to how people devalue themselves.

Identity isn't only about how we're perceived but also how we perceive the world. Will we become positive forces in the world, or will we remain silent wallflowers, afraid to voice opinions in fear that we don't matter?

Ridicule is painful. I know this from my experiences as a child. I know because the memories stayed with me for more than the first few decades of my life. I was fortunate enough to develop strong instincts and self-awareness, and I made some close friends who helped me come out of my shell. I also looked for a way to turn the negative things in my life into positives. This helped me immensely in getting through the rough moments.

I learned many things about life just from watching movies. When I was younger, my adoration for movie stars taught me some good life lessons. I paid attention to everything I learned and always focused on pulling a positive message from the things I read and watched.

My idol was and still is Barbra Streisand. I had a weakness for love stories, and when the breakups happened in movies, I would cry as though it was my heart being broken. I suspect that many of my overwhelming emotions stemmed from the uncertainty I had grown up with, living in a broken home, but movies gave me more than just sadness—I picked out some interesting lines from those stories, lines I took as values to live by.

In my favorite movie, *Funny Girl*, Streisand played Fanny Brice, a woman who saw herself as awkward but was determined to become a singer with the Ziegfeld Follies. I identified with her on so many levels. Fanny did manage to get through, earning her claim to fame. I had loved Barbra since I was a child and aspired to sing like her. I thought she was beautiful, and I couldn't help but wonder if Barbra herself was projecting some of her own insecurities through Fanny's character. I didn't notice Fanny Brice, I saw only Streisand.

In the movie, Fanny made fun of herself. In the scene where she was to sing a bridal number while portraying herself as a beautiful bride, she couldn't bring herself to dress the part. She didn't consider herself beautiful. She had a wonderful sense of humor, and instead, she took it upon herself to change her appearance for the number. Fanny came out looking overly pregnant with a big pillow stuffed up her gown. The audience loved it. Mr. Ziegfeld was mortified and reamed her out afterward for turning a beautiful scene into a comedy. Fanny simply replied that she felt inadequate singing a song about how beautiful she was, and she decided that by pulling off that stunt, the audience would laugh with her and not at her.

That scene stuck with me from that moment on. It became my inspiration to overcome my own inhibitions about my appearance. I had been gifted with a sense of humor but had kept it hidden while growing up because I wasn't confident enough to allow the extrovert in me to show.

It wasn't long after seeing that movie that I became more comfortable in my own skin, and this allowed my personality to peek out. My love for reading books and watching movies played a big part in forming and asserting my identity. All I had ever wanted was to be liked and accepted. By learning to climb my way around my flaws and turn them into positives, and by capitalizing on my sense of humor, I quashed my feelings of insecurity.

Section 2: Relationships

Alone Versus Lonely

Being alone is often misconstrued as being lonely, but it affords an independence I've learned to treasure through the years. When I was a child filled with insecurity and longing for emotional attention, I felt alone. Even as I grew into a teen, making several friends, my introverted state didn't allow me to talk about anything of personal significance with anyone. I felt alone even when I was among people. But when I moved away from home, my newfound freedom, and the deep connections I formed with others helped me grow into myself and shed my inhibitions. With my newly acquired friends helping to build my confidence and making me feel that what I had to say was important, I became the happy, extroverted person I had always known resided within me.

I lived on my own for many years, and I loved it. Sure, I had tons of friends and plenty of romantic relationships, but I loved my independence and began to treasure the time I spent alone. When I was alone, it was because I chose to be. Perhaps I had done it so well as a child that I was quite all right being alone. In fact, I believe all that early independence played a part in my youthful decision to choose not to marry. One can get quite used to living life exactly how she wants to, without someone telling her what she can and cannot do. When I finally got married, later in life, I was set in my ways, and I knew what I wanted out of life by then, which made it harder to adapt to a committed relationship.

At that point, I wasn't going to settle for anything short of what I expected from a relationship, including the maintenance of my independence. For me to make a huge commitment to marriage, there had to be unconditional love and acceptance for my beliefs and passions. Above all, I needed to maintain my freedom to speak my opinions without anyone telling me to hush up. I knew that was a tall order for many men to comply with, but I didn't need a man to complete me. I had grown secure within myself.

My life was full. I had a good career and eventually owned my own home. If I was ever going to succumb to marriage, it would be for love, compassion, and respect. I wanted to be with someone who would allow me to continue to grow, someone who would be happy for my accomplishments instead of stunting my growth or hindering me on my path. It took a big man to fill those shoes, but I found him. I know who I am, and when my husband doesn't understand me, he lets me be, trusts my instincts, and supports my decisions. This is a healthy foundation for a relationship.

Coming from a life of independence, I never wanted to surrender my alone time. You know those times when we may not feel like talking, or we may just feel like getting lost in a TV show or a good book? I also believe in getting away with a girlfriend occasionally for a timeout. I acquired all these preferences while living on my own, and as long as I was giving one hundred percent in my marriage, I could still enjoy doing the things I had always enjoyed. Many times when my husband is home, I'm working or writing, and he gives me my space and never complains. Sometimes I get so lost in the zone that I don't want to stop and make dinner—and that's still okay with him.

Everything my husband gives me, all the freedoms he affords me, propels me to give back more. When you can reciprocate kindness with someone, it becomes a very natural gesture. Our human instincts are that like brings like, and discord breeds only more discord.

I'm not lonely when I'm in my alone space, but it's important to make time to do things together, and we do enjoy one another's company. Living on one's own doesn't necessarily mean one is lonely, and one can be part of a couple without losing her independence.

Alternatively, there are people who, although surrounded by others, still feel lonely, just as I did as a child. If we don't have nurturing people in our lives who genuinely care about our thoughts and feelings, we will no doubt feel lonely. It's under these circumstances that we should re-evaluate what we need to fulfill our happiness and take strides to better our relationships.

As we grow older and our lives seem busy and full of responsibilities, we long for and appreciate a sacred timeout. Besides wanting it, we need it. We all need the space to take a breather and do the things we personally enjoy for relaxation. Timeouts also allow us to assess events in our lives and re-evaluate, reflecting on ourselves. A little "me time" is good for the soul.

Sometimes I may just want to relax, or I may feel like diving into a little project around the house. I enjoy the freedom of having time to myself. Life is busy for everyone, with its daily demands, and it seems as though our to-do lists are never ending, because that's life. Tasks never seem to end, but life does, so embrace your solo moments!

What's the Attraction?

Do you ever wonder why we gravitate to certain types of partners? Is it because we randomly meet people and connect with them, or are most of us in search of the perfect partners, not willing to settle for anything less than our ideal mates? I dare not say that anyone is perfect. We all have flaws, and sometimes we choose the wrong partners for a number of reasons. Perhaps we've spent a long time searching for meaningful relationships and we're tired of being alone, so we settle.

When we find the opportunity to hook up with someone, we may be willing to forego some of our requirements in a mate, grateful that we've finally met someone. Or maybe we only see the qualities we like in that person and tend to overlook the things we don't? Either way, I think these choices are a recipe for disaster in the long term. I can speak from experience about this because I too once fell into this situation.

I can say with certainty that I was better off being alone than allowing myself to succumb to a partner I abhorred. I allowed myself to settle for a relationship with a charming, nice-looking guy who I continued to go out with while trying to ignore my inner knowledge that there were just some things I didn't like about him. I thought I was being too picky, and as it had been a few years since I allowed myself to get involved with someone, I thought perhaps I was being too selective and had to give the guy a chance. Well, one thing led to another, and before I knew it, I was trapped in a bad relationship.

When someone breaks your spirit, it's not a good thing. I didn't just let a few of my standards fall by the wayside, I settled for a relationship that didn't adhere to my values. I saw this more and more as the relationship progressed. My love for laughter was smothered, and my optimistic outlook on life darkened.

That relationship was costly. It took up some of the best years of my life, but I learned a lot from it, and it only served to reinforce my strength and my decision never to allow myself to settle half-heartedly for things again. I learned that I would never let anyone prevent me from being who I was. I learned to value my personal freedom much more highly once I got out of that relationship. When I finally chose to marry a few years later, I realized the qualities I needed and wanted in a man before making a life commitment.

My decisions and the lessons of my past led me to choose the right partner with whom to share a happy marriage. If we don't learn to stand up and live for what we believe in, and if we allow ourselves to be bulldozed by our partners, by them not respecting our thoughts and preferences, we will eventually be left emotionally unfulfilled.

We have the ability to attract many suitors, whether through our looks, our dispositions, or our intelligence. We can meet people anywhere, and this can happen when we least expect it. Heck, I even meet people in the grocery store. Sometimes we may not be aware that our body language exudes a lot about our personalities. I know that my persona always radiates happiness. I smile at people when I pass them or find them glancing at me. This opens a door to making someone feel comfortable, signaling that I'm friendly.

Often when I'm grocery shopping, a man or woman will approach me out of the blue, asking me if I've tried a particular item I may be holding at the time. More often than not, I'll be approached and asked where someone can find a particular product. It sometimes leaves me wondering if I look like the official greeter of the store! I usually just chuckle and take it in stride that people feel comfortable talking to me. I project approachability. People can sense from my disposition and body language that I'm friendly, and they feel comfortable enough to approach me and ask questions.

The people we're initially attracted to or gravitate toward are usually decided by our morals and the standards we strongly hold. Our younger experiences usually instill in us what we crave in an ideal mate. As we grow and learn about ourselves, we begin to discover the qualities that appeal to us in a meaningful relationship. The values and traits we look for in a potential partner often stem from the comfort we felt around people we grew up with, people who made us feel loved and special.

Perhaps we held a fondness for someone special when we were younger, and quite possibly there were people we secretly admired. Those people could have been people who crossed our paths, TV personalities, or simply people we regarded as Prince Charming types, people we dreamed of as our ideal mates. Maybe we're physically attracted to muscular guys because we watched a lot of *Baywatch*? Or maybe we're attracted to the geeky guys because we're the studious, bookworm types? We tend to cling to the comfort we feel from certain people. Whether real or imagined, what we found appealing remains in our memories.

Growing up surrounded by negative influences can also lead us into choosing inappropriate mates if we fail to acknowledge that the people we're influenced by were not positive forces in our lives. If we continue to go on without realizing how destructive those influences were, we never grow and learn from them. Our fragile egos are especially delicate when we're young, when the seeds of the future are planted in us. The key to happiness is recognizing the negative influences in our lives and searching for ways to change them into positives.

Our tastes and desires can ultimately change as we mature,

but more often than not, our initial attractions stem from values we see in the people we admired or fantasized about as children. For some of us, attraction comes easily when people pay us attention—while our insecurities plague us and we ask ourselves, "Am I good enough for someone to want me?" This was a perpetual question I found myself asking. I questioned my looks, my body type, and my worth.

I'm quite sure, when I take a hard look at my own patterns in life and the choices I've made concerning men, that my preference for older men definitely has something to do with the love I had for my father. I often heard the term "daddy complex" used when friends or family were scrutinizing my choices in men.

The Daddy Complex

A long time ago, there was a stigma that I'm sure still lingers today. When a woman is seen with an older man, a common reaction is "What does she see in him? She must be out for his money." Many people suggest that women in relationships with older men are trying to reinvent the relationships they had with their fathers.

In my experience, I can say with certainty that it was never about money—but I can't say that my attraction to older men didn't stem from the love I had for my father, the one man who loved me unconditionally when I was young.

Growing up, I spent more time around adults than I did with children. As an awkward child and teenager, with little self-esteem, it was comforting for me when a male adult was kind to me and paid me attention. Through the years, my mother's many male friends would sometimes compliment me and indulge me with conversation during their visits. I wasn't aware at the time whether they were sincere or perhaps just engaging in small talk to get into my mother's good graces, but those times gave me some breadcrumbs of excitement, making me feel important. Those were quite possibly the beginnings of my beliefs that I was interesting enough for someone to pay any attention to. I'm not a psychoanalyst, but it's always easier to find answers after things have played out.

I became more comfortable around adults than around boys my own age. It occurred to me that boys my age were essentially attracted to physical appearance, while older men actually enjoyed talking with me and showed interest in what I had to say. As I grew well into my teens, I began to notice that I was attracted to older men.

In junior high, I developed secret crushes on some of my teachers, not the students. If I try to dissect why I felt this way, what comes to mind is my need for understanding and compassion. Those two things were what I most hungered for as a child. For me, it was never about how hunky a guy was or what a great physique he had. With my teachers, it was about the attention I received when merely asking a question and receiving an explanation with patience and a smile.

I often stayed back in class for a few minutes when the period ended to ask for extra help on some subject I wasn't clear about. I was afraid to put my hand up in class, fearing that my question was stupid and kids might laugh at me. I looked at those after-class times as special moments and was thrilled that someone as important as a teacher was spending one-on-one time with me to satisfy my questions.

The attractions I felt had nothing to do with sexual fantasies. They were fueled by the fondness I developed for my teachers, by the attention I craved. I somehow connected better with men. I didn't have a lot of friends, and I was very selective about who I allowed into my life. I was quite an introvert, the polar opposite of the person I kept hidden within myself and wouldn't divulge until I moved away from home. I always knew I had a lot to say and give, but while growing up, I didn't have the nerve to voice my thoughts or ask questions to anyone except my father.

My dad was always amused at the things I'd say and the stories I told him. He always had faith that my big personality, which I had kept hidden, would one day emerge when I'd be set free.

Shortly after I moved away from home, I befriended a man in a cafe I frequented, and we developed a deep friendship. He taught me a lot about the world and people and made me feel special and smart. Somewhere along the way, I fell in love with him. He was much older than I was, and he was crazy about me. His being married was so irrelevant to me at the time because marriage was the furthest thing from my mind. I was just happy to be comfortable with someone I could bear my soul to and feel so unconditionally loved by. He thought I was beautiful, and he made me feel beautiful, too.

As the years progressed and I entered into new relationships, my attraction to older men never faltered. As I finally began to grow into myself and accepted my looks, I gained the attention of other men, but just as I had always been selective with my female friends, I was just as fussy about the men I chose to date.

No two men I dated ever shared the same profile in the looks department. Some were incredibly handsome, and some provoked people to question, "What are you doing with him? He's not even good looking." For me, good looks stemmed from the soul. The initial attraction for me lay in a certain look in a man's eyes or the way he smiled. I needed to sense kindness. I needed someone with an open heart to accept me for all that I was.

I had many suitors, and it's human nature for a male to be initially attracted physically, but it was necessary for me that a man love me for who I was and not underestimate my intelligence, trying to court me in the hopes that I could become another notch on his bedpost.

I was so adamant in my need for respect. I'm sure that being a misunderstood and emotionally neglected child played a huge part in the attention I was seeking and the standards I held. It had become apparent to me that younger guys couldn't wait to dive into the sack, whereas older guys, who may have had the same hopes on the backburner, really did enjoy the act of dating and stimulating conversation. If a man couldn't arouse me mentally and emotionally, there was no chance that I was going to have sex with him. I had never been interested in the proverbial one-night stand.

My ideas about relationships worked out well for me. Although my theory about seeing married men bombed out, I learned some important lessons. My ventures into relationships were all learning experiences. I had no prior experience and no dating advice to carry with me. I lived every day as though it was a new day, with no anticipation of change, hurt, or heartache. When we're young, we don't seem to worry about tomorrow.

I thought I had the map of my life all laid out. I decided I never wanted to be married, and I supposed, during those times, that going out with a married man wasn't a problem for me because I wasn't looking to get tied down. I was young, and so was my thinking. I eventually learned a hard lesson from choosing those relationships, and it put an end to my "dating married men" theory. Later in life, I met my husband, who is, in fact, twenty years older than I am. Some things don't change.

In summation, perhaps my preference for older men did evolve from the relationship I had with my father. Perhaps I was seeking the attention and comfort I had needed as a child, wanting to be understood and appreciated. I had been obsessed with that need since I was young, but I didn't realize why until I was older and began reassessing my childhood.

Self-Worth, Insecurities, and Attractions

The summer before I moved away from home, my dad sent me to Europe. The trip was a high-school graduation gift. I was eighteen, but my desire to explore the world had already set in, and I looked forward to escaping my unhappy home life. I went on an organized six-week tour of five countries, complete with a tour organizer and twenty-three others ranging from age eighteen to twenty-three. We first flew from Toronto to New York to pick up the American passengers who were joining the tour.

The adventure opened my eyes to different cultures and my first real experience with male attention. It was an opportunity for me to form new friendships and indulge in my great love for shopping. I was at a crossroads during that time, getting ready to move away from home while just having finished high school, struggling to accept my flaws and find my identity. On that trip, I began to find my voice, and my hidden extroverted personality began to emerge. I was so excited to be on the other side of the world, meeting new people. It was a big step up from the small perimeters of the life I had known.

By that time, I had become ultra fashion conscious. I experimented with style, and I loved to dress up, but I developed a strategy for everything I wore. I wanted to enhance my better features and keep camouflaged what I didn't like about myself. I was fairly chunky at that time and inwardly humiliated by my weight. I was extremely self-conscious about flaunting my flaws for the world to see, and I had learned to sacrifice comfort for the sake of my vanity.

At the time, I still had long blond hair. My facial features had begun to form into some semblance of pretty, with my high cheekbones and my almond-shaped green eyes. Although I was still in my blue eye shadow phase, I thought I put myself together reasonably well. I had an affinity for skirts at the time.

My logic told me skirts were more flattering than pants, which called attention to my large thighs. Wearing high heels always, at any cost, had also become an integral part of my wardrobe strategy by that point.

Only I would go to Europe to travel through ruins and sightsee in high heels. All the other people on the tour comfortably strode along up and down hills, stairs, and broken cobblestone walkways with their sneakers on. Did I stand out like a sore thumb? Of course I did! But my vanity and insecurities were fueled by my own reverse psychology. I was sure that people thought I dressed this way to seek attention, when in fact it was for the contrary. I dressed this way so I wouldn't have to reveal my less flattering features, unaware that I was in fact attracting attention to myself with my sometimes inappropriate attire. But, being a jovial person who loved to make people laugh, I never encountered any harmful ridicule, mostly because I was always the first to comment on my own bizarre appearance. I feared being ridiculed, so, drawing on my memories of Fanny Brice, I would be the first to make jokes about myself.

I established close bonds with two of the guys on the tour, Henry and Howard. We became like the three musketeers. Most of what I remember was constant laughter with us. The tour's especially difficult portion occurred when we arrived in Israel. It was very hot, and we toured many ruins—Bethlehem, Masada, and other places. Walking through the rubble and climbing steep hills in the sometimes 130-degree temperatures, complete with my high heels, had Henry and Howard coming to my aid several times to help drag me up those hills. All the while, we'd be doubled over in laughter because of how crazy I was, wearing my heels. We also had to stay on a Kibbutz for three days—not something I wanted to do, but I was informed it was a mandatory part of the tour.

Working in the fields, picking weeds at five in the morning in my heels, was not a fun experience. That was the job I had been assigned, and it was not acceptable to the girly girl I was.

I also realized why the Arabs wore the veiled head garb—it was so bloody hot! Shading one's head became an instant reflex to defend against the sweltering heat from the sun beating down on us. The guys instinctively took off their T-shirts and wrapped them around their heads. Despite all my whining and complaining, I had never laughed so hard in my entire life.

While we were touring Israel, we had the same bus driver, Jack, for the two-week duration. Maybe it was my blond hair, or perhaps it may have been the way I dressed or my constant provision of entertainment and laughter, but I often caught Jack staring at me from his rear-view mirror. He'd often confront me at our lunch-time pit stops, and we'd share broken English and mistranslated conversations. Then he tried to kiss me. While I had no attraction to him, I was flattered by his attention, and he made me feel special. It was the beginning of my realization that men were now paying attention to me.

Ironically, when we were in Italy, I encountered another bus-driver attraction with Roberto. Italy, with its reputation for romantic men, captivated me, and my love for the country and the culture stayed with me. (When I moved away from home, my social circles comprised mainly Italians!) All the fantasies I imagined about chivalry and romanticism became a reality for me when I was in Italy.

The ambiance of that country sang romance to me. I actually had my bum pinched in front of the Trevi Fountain in Rome, and instead of finding it invasive, I was flattered. I had heard that was a custom at the time if a man was attracted to you. That was definitely a different time.

Roberto was our driver for the week we spent touring Venice, Rome, and Florence. He was a quiet man who spoke with his deep, dark eyes. He had taken a shining to me, and while everyone took his or her own luggage from the undercarriage of the bus at each new hotel we arrived at, Roberto always insisted on carrying mine for me. He was very handsome with his dark wavy hair and Mediterranean features, very seductive.

He spoke barely a word of English, but we somehow shared conversations using many hand signals (and the Italians are known for talking with their hands!) during our daily pit stops for lunch. I never saw him after the day ended. No matter how attracted I was to him, I knew enough not to venture out of my hotel room in a strange country.

We kissed a lot, and I found myself so caught up in the epitome of romanticism. When we left Italy, Roberto asked for my address so he could write to me. He wrote me beautiful letters for two years after that trip. I remember thinking he must have had someone translate them for him. I got so excited when I received his letters. Our relationship was like a secret fantasy I didn't share with anyone. Although it was a vacation romance, he made me feel special and his attraction to me helped me to acknowledge my self-worth. I realized that my weight didn't have to condemn me as a wallflower. My spirit and personality naturally attracted friends and suitors.

I really believe that it was during that summer vacation, on my own in the big world, that I began to see myself how others saw me. Before that trip, I had lived mostly inside my own head. With no encouragement growing up, I wasn't aware of my worth and had low self-esteem.

Although I strived to acquire a sense of style so I could feel comfortable in public, and I wanted to be happy, I hadn't previously had the opportunity because I was so insecure and afraid of exposing my personality. I was afraid of how others would perceive me. I kept my big personality wrapped up within, without knowing how to exercise it. When I found myself alone in the world, I began to recognize who and how I wanted to be. I became quite a chatterbox and found it easy to form friendships. I acquired the ability to make people laugh, and I no longer felt like the odd man out. Nobody made fun of me. Most importantly, I no longer felt awkward and out of place.

Relationships and Self-Worth

When it comes to relationships, our self-esteem plays a major part in how we project ourselves. When we first seek out a suitor, we project ourselves a certain way, and as relationships develop, we may find ourselves deviating from the people we are to the people our partners prefer us to be. If we dwell on our critical selves when dating, we may potentially lose the interest of a possible connection or quite possibly attract someone with incompatible values. Either way, this isn't a positive union. Don't get me wrong: I'm not saying beautiful women can't get away with a lot more, but in the end, the results will inevitably be the same.

Plenty of men have the tendency to be shallow when it comes to physical beauty, leaving them unprepared for the discovery that they may not be attracted to the person underneath that beauty.

Take, for example, the type of woman who constantly criticizes herself in front of others, picking herself apart, always desperately seeking validation. A man can easily be taken in with what he likes about the physical features of this woman, feeling as though he can either overlook her other flaws or coddle her, stroking her weak ego to make her feel better and thus boosting his own ego. Let's presume they continue on into a relationship and perhaps even into marriage, but after some time has passed, the man grows weary of hearing the same criticisms and tires of having to constantly uplift the woman's ego. This is a perfect example of initial physical attraction not holding strong enough to cement the relationship. Nobody is going to grow from this behaviour. Eventually, the man will tire of all the mental work involved.

If we're in a relationship with someone we can't grow with or receive emotional support from, that relationship is going to grow stale. Men also seek emotional support for themselves. Eventually, people who are emotionally unfulfilled by their relationships will acquire a roving eye. Physical appearance, in the long haul, is not enough on its own for people to bond emotionally.

Confidence takes us a long way in life, although it can sometimes take us a lifetime to build. When we're in healthy relationships, we're able to talk about anything with our partners. We should be made to feel that it's okay to voice our opinions. If we're feeling inadequate and deflated at times, our partners should be there to encourage us, not to criticize us.

Too many times we fall for the wrong types of partners because we are attracted to a certain quality while overlooking the ones we don't like. If those overlooked qualities are major character flaws, they're no doubt going to bite us down the road. This is why it's essential that we attract the right types of mates. If we can be our own true selves when meeting new potential partners, then we won't have to pretend to be people we're not as the relationships progress. In the same vein, if we accept relationships that become unhealthy, we owe it to ourselves to get the hell out. If a bad situation isn't recognized or repaired, it's only going to get worse.

Flirtation

The age-old practice of flirting is an amorous behavior with the intent of vying for attention, sometimes with sexual connotations. Flirting can have different meanings and intentions depending on the desired result. Some may flirt to capture the attention of the object of their affections. Others may flirt with no particular intention other than to attract attention for self-gratification, for superiority. Some people flirt for the sheer thrill of the conquest, with no regard for the conquest's feelings.

Essentially, we flirt in hopes of engaging a particular person's attention. The means chosen to attract such attentions are plentiful. In past decades, flirting usually involved a woman batting her eyelashes at a targeted suitor or perhaps putting a wiggle in her walk, gently sashaying her hips with every step.

Fast-forwarding to modern times, women use a multitude of methods to flirt. Anything from flashing a sexy smile, to staring provocatively, to crossing one's legs seductively are methods of flirting. Wearing sexy attire, such as miniskirts and low-cut tops, will also provoke an onlooker's attention. Most women have an arsenal of tactics they can use to be flirtatious. In our modern age of technology, we have advanced to the art of sexting—typing seductive text messages on our smartphones to arouse the attentions of the one we desire.

Why we flirt is personal. Most often, there's a specific target in mind for our flirtatious actions, but flirting is also used as a means of self-satisfaction, whether selfishly or out of sincerity. If you strip the logic down to its core, both reasons boil down to one. We all have faults, whether recognized or not—Achilles' heels likely stemming from incidents in our younger lives. We may be seeking the affection or attention we were previously denied. We may use flirtation to seek approval for ourselves, to validate ourselves, to tell ourselves that we're worthy, socially acceptable, or desirable. Our egos may lead us to believe that we have to be the object of someone's attentions to quantify our sexualities.

When women are confident, they can easily reflect that in their mannerisms, having an innate ability to flirt effortlessly.

Self-confidence is a major attraction. Some women possess the ability to walk into a room and find themselves the object of attention, whether from men or women. The gift of being self-assured overshadows insecurities and allows us to stand or walk proudly, smile at everyone, and converse with people at different levels. These traits alone are enough to attract interest.

Imagine those people who strive to appear as someone they're not. Say, for example, that a woman sets out for an evening to go to a fancy party with a goal in mind to snag a potential suitor of a certain caliber—a man she sees as being totally out of her league, financially or intellectually. This usually means that woman doesn't have confidence in herself, because she can't envision herself with a man of a certain status. It could also mean that this woman doesn't have faith in herself or her own appearance or worth. Perhaps she may be financially out of sorts. If this woman decides to go to this party with the intent of portraying herself as someone she's not, what could the repercussions be?

What if she borrows a dress from a friend to doll herself up, and she goes to the party and meets someone interesting, and she chooses to introduce herself as someone she's not? She makes up a profession and gloats about a wonderful vacation she's just returned from in her imagination. She's clever and has armed herself with knowledge from stories she's heard and information she's gotten off the Internet. She manages to capture the attention of an interesting man with a good education and a successful business. Let's say they begin dating soon after, and then what? How long can the charade continue? How many times can this woman borrow clothes and keep a conversation going about things she only pretends to know before he catches on and finds that he has been deceived?

Some people can pull off a caper like this, but rarely forever. It may take people a while to comprehend others' complexities, but eventually, we have to find out who our partners really are. It's difficult to build trust on a relationship that begins in deceit.

If our example woman had taken the opposite approach, going to that same party and meeting that same man under different circumstances, the situation would have unfolded quite differently.

If we can learn to work on our self-confidence and present ourselves in public as our true selves, we can have much more positive results. Working on ourselves is not only about our physical appearance, it's about having a positive frame of mind and educating ourselves by reading books, following current events, and getting involved in activities or hobbies that interest us and help expand our minds. This in turn gives us more confidence to contribute to conversations upon meeting new people.

We don't have to be world travelers, and we don't have to have university degrees beside our names to be worthy of anyone. We all have our own unique qualities, and we must learn to exercise them to their fullest potential. Greeting people with a smile and adding a little humor when speaking allows positivity to shine in our personalities. These steps are a great help in attracting people who will want to get to know us. Positivity attracts positivity.

It's much easier to go through life being who we are than to pretend to be someone we're not. That can become exhausting day after day, and eventually, we'll be caught off guard at some point, and all that will remain is a tarred reputation. We should never have to doubt who we are. We need to reach deep inside ourselves to pull out our best qualities and show what we have to offer. We are all worthy of being loved. We all have our own individual unique qualities. We only have to recognize them.

Contrary to popular belief, people aren't solely attracted to physical godlike beauty. Yes, initially that may be an attention grabber, but if that person has nothing else to offer by way of kindness, compassion, or common sense—or if he or she is devoid of a pleasant personality altogether—the attraction will eventually fizzle out. That's real life. The types of people who live their lives with the sole purpose of believing that the world should revolve around them because of their beauty are commonly referred to as narcissists. I'm quite familiar with that type of personality, and I wrote about it in my earlier book *Conflicted Hearts*. The subject was my own mother.

As I matured and began to see my mother for who she really was, beyond her beauty, I made it my business not to become like her. We're all products of our environments, and there are really only two ways to grow from our upbringings. We either carry on in a manner we're familiar with, or we do everything in our power to become the opposite. Yes, I strived to look my best to conquer my feelings of inadequacy, but I never wanted to become a self-centered person who groomed herself to use her looks to manipulate people for her own good. I spent years studying my mother to try to understand what had spurred her ego, what had caused her to become so manipulative.

We shouldn't aspire to be anything but our true authentic selves. The world is full of beautiful women, but true beauty always stems from within. We all know physical beauty doesn't last forever. This is something many people don't consider about the future, only concerned about what they can obtain with their looks in the now. Granted, people are inherently attracted to physical beauty initially, but as time passes, if there's nothing beautiful to accompany a person's physical attributes, people will stop paying attention. Projecting inner beauty can take us a lot further through life in a positive way. It doesn't wither with age, and it draws a healthy sort of attention.

Abuse

Abuse comes in many forms, and often it isn't recognized. Many women endure abuse not only physically but also mentally and emotionally. Other women may not even be aware they're being abused. Abuse is a power that leaves us feeling defenceless and weakened as we continue to succumb to it. Abuse can happen to anyone—male, female, children, and animals—but since this book is geared toward women's issues, I'm going to focus on abusive tactics used against women.

Too many women are abused every single day. Sadly, some of these women aren't even aware they are living under abusive situations because they have endured so long that they learn to accept it as their standard of living. The tactics used to abuse come in many forms. Belittling of character, name-calling, threats, and mean-spirited actions are just a few.

It's interesting to know just how delicate our psyches are. Mere words can make us feel demeaned, valueless, and inadequate. After suffering these insults for a long time, we lose our self-esteem and devalue ourselves. Repeatedly subjecting ourselves to the abuse, unaware of what's really happening to us, we stay in those situations instead of seeking a way out. Eventually, the abuse does take its toll on our self-esteem, and we become brainwashed. We get so accustomed to the constant belittling that it puts us in a depression or worse. Sometimes we become so changed that we don't even realize we're depressed.

I'll speak frankly about this deflation of self-esteem because I've lived through it. Many years ago, I was one of those victims. Without going into great detail about what I endured, I'll focus on the effects it had on me.

I was once in a long relationship with an abuser. I was younger, and although at the beginning of the relationship I questioned some of his behavior, I chose to overlook it. Several red flags were presented to me that I should have paid heed to. His sporadic temper created many disagreements over insignificant things. By that time in my life, I was a happy, free-spirited girl who had already accomplished so much to get myself in a place where I was satisfied with who I had become. I loved to laugh and had the gift of easily making others laugh. But as time went by in this relationship, I noticed that I was no longer joyful. I became very cautious about every word I spoke and everything I did around him so as not to leave anything for him to criticize me for.

After some time passed and I was very aware of my circumstances, I thought I could handle him—I could fix him. How many of us women have been in that position where we feel like the caregivers, wanting to make things better, make our partners better? I know the answer—many. Instead of us paying heed to our internal warnings and getting the hell out, we stay. Why do we stay? It becomes a mission for us to fix, help, nurture, and support these men. Why this is, I'm not sure. Perhaps it's our nature as women to instinctively want to help.

Many of us feel we can take on anything, and perhaps others feel they have nowhere else to go. I can say with certainty that staying is never the right decision, no matter what the alternatives. After hanging around too long, it gets more difficult to get out. We begin to feel emotionally compelled to stay, and many times, we're financially dependent on these people. But these reasons are just not good enough reasons to hang around.

In my predicament, he demeaned me whenever he was angry. He'd flash a pointed index finger in my face and tell me what I was and wasn't going to do. If he didn't care for the dinner menu I had chosen (and I'm a good cook), he threw the plate and the food on the floor. He raised his hand to me repeatedly and threw me into a few walls. His alcoholism escalated in those moments. After too much time passed, I felt trapped and didn't know my way out. I became silent around him to avoid arguments, and I began going out whenever he was home to maintain some of my sanity. I was afraid to confront him and ask him to leave. I was praying that if I ignored him long enough, he would leave on his own accord. That turned out to be a very long process, and while the time passed, friends and family constantly urged me to make him leave *my* home.

I was living in a hell, and my self-esteem was crushed. I had been an attractive, vibrant young woman with a big personality and a grand sense of humor. I was an optimist, always looking for the bright side, but there was no longer any bright side. My self-esteem had been deflated and belittled for so long that it had changed me. I was so caught up in it that I didn't realize how damaged I had become. My friends and family kept reminding me that I was no longer the person they had known. My zest for life had been quashed. The laughter in my eyes had disappeared. I can say now that I was depressed without even realizing it.

I was more afraid to ask him to leave than I was to keep living under those conditions. I believed this was my own fault and punishment for not following my instincts from the beginning. He became jealous when I ignored him, spewing terrible names at me when he couldn't have my attention. When he regained his composure, he'd repeatedly apologize for his episodes and would try to win back my affections to no avail.

After years passed, he finally said he was leaving, and my heart sang. Only when it was nearing the time for him to leave did his final efforts to win me back, and my refusal, spur on one of the worst moments of my life. He had decided that if he couldn't have me, nobody else could. It was by the grace of God that I narrowly escaped his clutches and ran away.

Many elements of abuse took place in that relationship. I was naive to the signs. I wasn't aware that being talked down to and being emotionally threatened constituted abuse. I remained in a situation that ate away at my self-esteem and integrity. I was lost in an abyss of unrecognized depression, and for a long time, it was hard for me to get out of it.

Situations like mine are unfortunately very common. I knew it was wrong for me to stay, yet I couldn't see the way out, so it was easier to be complacent and just stay, almost feeling as though I deserved it. *Nobody* deserves to be abused! Because it's common for women to act as nurturers and caregivers and fixers, we can become victims, enslaved by our own conflictions. When we get in too deep, we're sometimes unable to grab the hands that reach out to help us. We can get so lost in our unhappiness that we can't seem to step out of the box and look in on ourselves to assess what's really happening.

We can compare the situation we're stuck in to that of a small child who's filled with curiosity and has yet to experience harm. The parent will tell them not to touch the stove because it's hot, yet the child is intrigued to find out what that really means. Not until they touch it and find out what it means to be harmed do they learn how bad it is. We tend to feel as though we need to do the escaping on our own terms. For the lucky few of us, we finally learn and break free. For those less fortunate, it can sometimes be too late.

I hope women will be able to relate to my experience, especially those of you who are still living under abusive circumstances. Don't touch that hot stove! Take the good advice offered by those who care about you, those who can look in and see what we sometimes become blind to.

Those who love us know us best. We must listen to our intuitions, and when we get those feelings of uncertainty, which are almost always correct, we have to take action not to become victims. Don't become a burn victim or anybody's punching bag—physically or mentally. Recognize the signs. Gauge your happiness factor. Pay attention to friends and loved ones. We're all special and unique, and we all deserve to be loved and appreciated. If we find that our partners are not worthy of our unique selves, we don't have to sell ourselves short. We don't need anyone to complete us. We need to love ourselves and respect ourselves before anyone else can. If there's fire, get out!

Negativity and Jealousy

It's a fact that negativity underlies our fears, and our guilt can play a big part in lowering our self-esteem. All of these traits connect with our levels of confidence, our strength of character, and our wellbeing. When we're constantly berated and not placing ourselves in positive circumstances, our energies are drained, which can hinder our ability to maintain a positive outlook on life.

Our fears can cripple us, holding us back from living our lives to the fullest. If we can take a moment to assess the things in our lives that aren't fulfilling us, and acknowledge what we feel is holding us back from what we wish to attain, we can begin to do some damage control. But if we choose to live our lives in the same unhappy patterns we've grown accustomed to without bothering to figure out the root cause of our problems, those problems become nearly impossible to overcome.

Sometimes facing our demons is hard, but that's the only way we can grow and become stronger. If we choose to remain complacent in our unhappiness, we become trapped there, and many people's lives remain stagnant because they fail to recognize why they're unsatisfied. It's all about taking the time to stop and listen, paying attention to the things that bother us instead of surrendering to them. If we can learn to take charge of ourselves and dig deep within to confront our fears and the injustices we face, we've made a great start, and we can then begin taking action to resolve our issues. We have to make a positive out of the negatives in order to become happy and emit our positivity, attracting similarly positive people into our lives.

Many women tend to surround themselves with negative people, resulting in damaging effects to their state of mind. We not only have the ability to inflict our own negativities, we sometimes find ourselves existing in negative surroundings because of the people we allow into our lives.

Take our moods, for example. Have you been in a great mood but found yourself in a conversation with someone who complained about everything, unable to show any happiness for any of the good things you share with them about your life? This type of negative force sucks out our enthusiasm like a leech.

This negative power can also linger from childhood. As children, we experience negative forces from incidents such as being reprimanded by a parent. In those moments when a parent is disciplining us, we immediately recoil and begin to feel inadequate about ourselves. If our actions are not explained to us with kindness, we're inclined to shrivel back in fear, a fear created by the negative approach used to rectify our wrongdoing. Incidents such as these are the beginnings of allowing negativity to steer our emotions.

The critics, naysayers, and unhappy people we allow into our lives have the ability to drain our good energy, leaving us feeling unoptimistic, as though they have let the air out of our enthusiasm. The influence of negativity becomes the barometer for our moods. People who constantly live under this umbrella of negativity get so used to it that they may not even realize where their happiness has gone. They've simply adjusted to living that way.

If a child grows up under those influences, he or she will more than likely grow into a person with low self-esteem and a lack of self-confidence. As we mature, we may also acquire friendships with people who have flawed perceptions of life and the world because of injustices that occurred in their own lives.

I'm the type of person who is very sensitive to energies. When I'm around negativity, I feel low. My compassion for others forces me to try to uplift them. If I try with my best efforts to no avail and don't walk away, I feel very uncomfortable and begin to question my own optimism. This is not a healthy situation. Some might call this a bad vibe. However we choose to label them, these energies are very contagious.

It has taken me half a lifetime to learn to walk away from those situations. For the first few decades of my life, the veil of negativity I felt in my mother's presence made me very uncomfortable. The unhappiness she felt in her own life reflected in the way she spoke to my siblings and me. Eventually, through enduring her moods for decades, I made a decision to walk away. Nobody should have to subject themselves to toxicity, whether from friends, family, or strangers.

Sometimes we make bad choices about who we allow into our personal lives. We may overlook someone's flaws or feel as though we can make them better. When it turns out we can't, we find ourselves unhappily saddled in those relationships. We tend to feel obligated to these friendships out of some sort of loyalty instead of allowing ourselves to walk away.

It took me decades before I realized I couldn't be the caretaker for everyone in my life. When I reached the point of feeling brought down by those negative influences, I learned to leave. It wasn't easy for me to do this as a young adult. At the time, I was much more susceptible to allowing negative thoughts and people into my life, and this took a toll on me emotionally. I discovered I wasn't feeling inner peace, yet I stayed in relationships for too long to avoid hurting others' feelings.

Dwelling on negative thoughts doesn't open us up to appreciating and attracting positive forces or people. When I began to reassess my life and discover ways to better myself, I read self-help books and uplifting stories about spirituality. One book in particular that made me begin to understand the effects of being positive was *The Law of Attraction,* by Esther and Jerry Hicks. It's a universal fact that we attract what we project and focus on.

The old cliché "Misery loves company" is profound. It equates well with the theory of the law of attraction. Just think about it for a moment. If we're miserable and go through life moping around with nothing positive to offer anyone in spirit or with words, what can we hope to attract? Most likely, we'll attract likeminded people—or possibly nobody at all. In the event that we may be lucky enough to attract a high-spirited person who extends a helping hand to us, it would be a blessing and a longshot.

As I began to learn to better my own self and find my happiness, I became that empathetic person who seemed to attract people whose emotional states were in need of repair. I found myself trying to instill gratefulness and trying to come up with solutions for their problems. I attracted these broken-winged people because of my high energy and my compassion, wanting to help these people instead of abandoning them because they were flawed. I learned a lot from those relationships, beginning with my own mother and then a man I was sure I could help repair.

I also acquired a few friendships along the way with women who sucked me dry emotionally. I allowed myself to become a sounding board—an Ann Landers, so to speak—and I made myself much too available for their every whim. I also noticed that with all of those relationships, it was always and only all about them. In those relationships, nobody ever asked me about how I was doing or how I felt. No concern was paid to me for the things that I would have liked to share.

Those were all learning relationships for me. When I finally found my own self-worth, with a lot of soul searching, I learned how to disengage from those types of people. I needed to be with people who didn't absorb all of my positivity, leaving me feeling empty and drained.

It's very easy for someone to tell you to just walk away, but when you're compassionate to people and considerate of their needs, it's not an easy thing to do. It's a process, and it takes time to adjust our attitudes and responses, but by working on me, through reading about and practicing positivity, I gained great insight and learned to analyze how I was behaving and why. With my newfound positive attitude, many good things and good people began to enter into my life.

In saying this, I'm not pretending that by becoming more positive and confident, you'll never encounter negative people, but you can learn to deal with them differently. With a newfound positivity and heightened self-esteem, we learn how to better assess situations and people and learn how to adapt ourselves to them without having to invite them into our lives.

If we can develop a better appreciation for ourselves and realize our own self-worth, we can learn how not to subject ourselves to negatives forces and situations that drain our emotional wellbeing.

The hardest part for me is letting go. Once I find myself in a situation I'm not comfortable in, it's not easy for me to walk away, feeling as though I've left someone wounded behind. I don't like discord or remorse, and I try to avoid hurting people's feelings at almost any cost. Many times in my life, my compassion has become my own downfall. I've allowed myself to get involved only to find out that escaping without offending the other person is difficult. I let my guilt over abandoning someone in need plague me—a guilty conscience that had been instilled in me as a child by my mother. This is something I have spent most of my life working to rid myself of.

As you begin to acquire your self-esteem, you'll find that becoming untangled from unhealthy situations becomes less of an issue. As you become less vulnerable to inviting those types of situations into your life, you'll find you no longer have to deal with walking away because you no longer allow those circumstances or people into your life.

Does Jealousy Equate to Insecurity?

Jealousy is an unhealthy emotion and doesn't only pertain to relationships of the heart. Many people have jealous tendencies over friendships and material things. Some people have a difficult time dealing with others who have things they desire or with people they feel come across as better than they do. Their unhappiness about the missing things in their lives can sometimes fuel their anger toward people who have something more or better than they do. It's natural for us to want nice things and to want to be satisfied with our physical appearance, but it isn't practical to think we'll all get what we want. Jealousy usually stems from insecurity. Our jealousies tend to grow from unfulfilled desires within ourselves.

I'm sure everyone has known at least one person afflicted with this crippling flaw. Many people aren't aware of their jealous ways because they're too busy comparing everyone else's lives to their own. After doing so for so long, they get stuck in the rut of the green-eyed monster.

People who feel this way have a difficult time being happy for others' accomplishments, possessions, and attributes. They'll sometimes project themselves as victims—"Woe is me! Why can't I have those things or be like that?" Some are canny, looking for fault in the good that someone else has.

Many afflicted with this syndrome have a hard time paying anyone a compliment for fear it will detract from their own fortune. Then there are those who actually become bullies in retaliation for their internal anger toward their perceived competition. In order to feel better about themselves, they belittle others. Those types of people have most likely had their own self-esteem deflated, or they've never developed a sense of self-acceptance. You have to love yourself before you're capable of being loved by others.

A fine line exists between loving someone and wanting to possess them. People who act possessive feel the need to covet what's theirs to ensure nobody tries to take it from them. They live within their insecurities, which propel them to act in a domineering manner. Perhaps they aren't happy with their appearance or status, so they try to protect what they do have in fear that their possessions and attributes may be easily overlooked for someone else more physically appealing. Thus, these people are left in an imagined state of threat. Isn't this what jealousy is all about? It's about something bigger or better than the things we are or have, which threatens our feelings of adequacy.

Jealousy can ruin relationships, not only those of the heart but friendships, as well. I've had my own share of girlfriends I've had to walk away from. I believe that if we are secure in ourselves, our relationships are more secure with others—unless, of course, someone gives us a tangible reason to question that relationship. I've also been involved in some friendships that have run their course.

Well over a decade ago, some friends of ours invited my husband and I to a New Year's party. The friends we joined at this party introduced us to another couple there. I'll refer to them as Mary and Tom. We chatted through the night, and I felt that we connected on some common ground.

Mary invited us to her home for dinner a few days later, and subsequently many more dinners, which became almost a weekly event. After getting to know them better, we found that we really liked Tom, but we were discovering how bossy and domineering Mary was, not only to Tom but also to anyone else in her presence.

I always liked to dress nice, and so did Mary. But I noticed that Mary had a big problem with other women if she felt they were attractive. I began to sense the daggers she was throwing at me with her cunning tongue.

Mary also had a tendency to remind everyone that everything she had and did was only the best. In fact, I felt that if I didn't compliment her enough to feed her hungry ego, I could sense her sarcasm growing. If we happened to be comparing recipes, she'd never fail to remind me that nobody could cook as well as she could. She would often nitpick with nonsensical statements such as "I don't like that you chew gum." When I told her that I chewed gum because I used to smoke and it helped to quash the cravings, she'd retort with "Well, I don't like people who smoke." By then, I'd usually be trying to end the conversation with no comment and a long silence. She had her ways of snarking about things and people she was envious of.

Mary was a nice-looking woman who carried a few extra pounds and didn't like that part of herself. It was obvious to anyone around her that she had a tough time offering a compliment to anyone, but that didn't stop her from tooting her own horn about how great everything she did and owned was in an effort to placate her competitive feelings.

One time, the four of us were in a restaurant and the maître d' was announcing the special of the day to us. I suggested to my husband that he might like to order it because the place we were in was famous for its veal parmesan. Mary popped herself into our conversation and said, "I don't care what restaurant you go to. Nobody makes it like I do."

I could feel Mary's need to have her ego stroked. I sensed her insecurity and narcissism. I knew I had to wean myself off that relationship because I couldn't stand being around self-centered people who could never be happy for others' accomplishments.

I invited Mary and Tom to my home. I had a lovely home, tastefully decorated. My home was very welcoming. Mary never paid me one compliment, not even "Your home is lovely," when she came over. Now, I don't need my ego stroked, but there's something to be said for people who can't say anything nice or even fake a compliment.

I love to compliment people and give credit where credit is due. If I ever walked into anyone's home, even if it wasn't to my taste, I'd still find something positive and nice to compliment that person for. I didn't need praising, but what if I did? What if I was an insecure person, worried about whether my things were nice enough to be socially accepted?

I had to wonder how many people Mary had made feel inferior in the past. This person had nothing positive to offer of herself in friendship except to have company over so that she could brag about her life and her cooking. She required an audience, not a friend. She needed to feel as though she was better than everyone else in order to feel good about herself.

Although the friendship had begun fast and furious, with the many invites for dinner, I ended it shortly after the dinner at my house. I had wanted out for quite some time but didn't want to hurt anyone's feelings. As luck would have it, Mary left me with good reason to end it.

I cooked up a feast at my little dinner soiree, and I had also invited a few other guests. Everyone had a lovely time. Great music played, the women drank wine, and the guys enjoyed their beer. If Mary noticed Tom and me in conversation, she was there like lightning. Nobody overindulged. It was a nice social gathering. My husband likes to entertain people when he's in a jovial party atmosphere: By "entertain," I mean that he likes to pretend to sing. I say pretend because he's tone-deaf and makes up his own words. Nonetheless, he sang a song, and everyone burst out laughing.

Two days later, Mary called me, reprimanding me and saying she didn't like people who got drunk. She told me that my husband had acted like a fool. Oh, yeah, she had barked up the wrong tree! I tore into her and finally told her what I thought about her and her petty jealousies. I asked her how she could dare insult my husband's happiness and accuse him of being drunk and misbehaving. I let her know that he hadn't been drunk, and even if he had been, it would have been none of her goddamned business. I hung up the phone and it was over. I just can't deal with miserable people who prey on other people's happiness.

I can safely say that I'm usually the first in a social event to compliment someone. I have no problem going up to a total stranger if I admire something they're wearing and letting them know. Whether I see a beautiful shade of lipstick or a fabulous outfit, I love to let people know how beautiful I think they are. The keyword here is "admire." It's quite healthy to admire something as opposed to being envious.

Giving a compliment to someone doesn't take anything away from myself. Whatever it is I may be admiring, it doesn't mean I don't have my own beautiful things or that whatever

I'm admiring makes my own things any less nice. Paying a compliment to someone is merely an expression, a way of letting someone know I appreciate the beauty in something he or she possesses. In doing so, I also make that person feel good. It's all positive.

I have great admiration for people who can freely give a compliment. It says a lot about their character. They aren't afraid to be kind and make someone's day. Sometimes it's just nice to be validated by others even though we may already feel good about ourselves.

People often compliment me, and it makes me feel good. The most special compliments I've received are the ones paid me by other women. It's common for a man to be attracted to the opposite sex and pay a compliment, whether sincerely or in hopes of establishing a potential connection, but a compliment from another woman can be so much more gratifying, especially to a self-criticizer. When we spend time putting ourselves together to go out somewhere yet are still feeling insecure about ourselves, a compliment can make us feel like we're okay and help calm our insecurities. Everyone loves to be complimented, whether to feed an ego or for a quick dose of inspiration.

I'm grateful that I am not, nor have I ever been, a jealous person—not with men, friendships, or possessions. I'm comfortable in my skin, and although I'm far from perfect, I make the best of who I am and what I have. I have an optimistic ability to see the beauty in many things, and I love to share a compliment where it's due. It can sometimes be tempting to get caught up in petty jealousies, but once we learn to accept ourselves and be grateful for everything we are and have to offer, we'll find there's nothing to be jealous about, because we all possess our own individual special qualities.

Instilled Guilt and Values

Our psyches are so fragile. The seeds planted in our minds at tender young ages become the roots of our beliefs, inhibitions, and insecurities, which are the hardest traits to conquer. Guilt has taken root deep in me since my childhood. When we're young, we may not recognize guilt as an emotion. We're more apt to identify its residual effects—fear, inferiority, and incompetence—all of which stem from the guilt instilled in us by a parent or close relative. Those feelings of guilt create unease within us, a fear of repercussions if we don't comply with threats, turning us into nervous children and consequently following us through our lives.

As young, impressionable children, we have only to believe what we're taught by our parents. We have no conception of, nor do we question, whether what we're taught is correct or valid because as children, that's all we know. Guilt comes with a foreboding that if we don't do what we're told, repercussions and/or punishment will follow. This was the norm when I was growing up.

My mother used guilt trips on my siblings and me throughout our childhoods. She would often use such threats such as "If you don't clean your room, I'll dump all of your clothes into the street." Another classic threat she used was "If you tell your father what you heard, you'll spend the summer in your room," or "If you don't do what I ask, you can't go to [insert whatever it was I was looking forward to at the time]." If I dared be defiant, an old favorite was "I'll smack you from here to New York."

As I grew, so did my fear of my mother's wrath. Her threats and blackmail held a lot of real estate in my head, pent-up fears that I would have to comply with her wishes or live with the guilty consequences. Even some of her good offerings came attached with a dangled carrot. If I did something she asked of me, she'd reward me with silence about a confidence I may have mistakenly shared with her. Those feelings of instilled guilt didn't end with childhood. They carried on throughout most of my life. This was the relationship I had with her. Is it any wonder that I grew up with self-esteem issues and developed a people-pleasing attitude?

My goal was to please from an early age to avoid being scolded and punished. My fears and self-esteem issues couldn't be resolved because I kept them to myself. I had no confidence to broach my questions and concerns with my self-absorbed mother. I had to find my own way through my dark thoughts and climb out or I'd be lost forever in my own critical opinions of myself, in my introverted state. I'm actually quite lucky I was a curious and very aware child. It prompted me to analyze my life and find a path to happiness and gratification instead of becoming another statistic—a depressed, lost individual. My perseverance to learn to be happy with myself was my own redeeming feature.

We really do all possess the ability to save ourselves. Sure, it can be a very long process, a continual work in progress, but I've learned to love myself and make the most of who I am. With all that said, I admit that erasing the guilt from my life has always been my biggest hurdle. I allowed my mother to hold power over me for most of my life, and even though I finally walked away, the guilt still occupies a place in my mind.

In my progress to move forward, I've learned a lot about overcoming my fears and embracing my accomplishments. Slowly, I conquered my insecurities and took back my power. It's very difficult to release guilt that we carry for most of our lives, and I think it could take more than a lifetime of therapy to overcome that guilt. But I have become stronger. I've learned to stand up for myself, and I'm no longer taken in by people who use guilt to obtain something for themselves. If we don't learn to recognize and rectify our damaged selves, the carnage will follow us through life and self-perpetuate, keeping us victims in all the relationships we develop.

"Mother knows best" is an old adage. We're conditioned to believe that our parents know best, and while experience can speak for a lot, the sheltered upbringings of past generations haven't necessarily impacted children positively. Many kids grow up with misconceptions of life because of parents who knew no better themselves, from their own upbringings.

Take prejudice, for example. Before the world evolved, racial slurs and prejudices abounded. So many races and nationalities were openly tagged with unflattering names. Even now, children growing up in prejudiced homes are instilled with this language, which sets the tone for the "Monkey see, monkey do" effect and teaches those children how to perceive other ethnicities and cultures. As those children get older, and hopefully wiser, they should question those prejudices and rise above the shallow beliefs of those who taught them. We need to take ownership of our own thoughts and begin judging people based on their morals and authenticity, not by the color of their skin or their country of origin.

I'm grateful that my inquisitive mind always kept me seeking answers to verify the things I was taught. I was the person who always needed proof, the eternal asker of why.

I grew up in a sheltered world with its share of prejudice. My father's parents were Orthodox Jews, though we weren't raised as such. They were pretty strict about trying to hammer into me their views of how Jewish children should be raised. My parents weren't religious, and my mother was Jewish only on her father's side and therefore didn't have much insight into the religion—yet she mimicked those societal values to my siblings and me, and she used to threaten me as a teen that I could only date Jewish guys. How ironic that became, because the more I grew into my social circles and myself, I realized I had no interest in dating Jewish guys. I couldn't lock myself into a society that didn't resonate with my personal preferences, which had more to do with culture and spirituality than religious beliefs.

I did a lot of reading on World War II, Judaism, and Catholicism to educate myself on religion and the Holocaust. My grandparents cursed the Germans for killing six million Jews, while I learned the difference between Germans and Nazis and didn't categorize them all under the same umbrella. In fact, I wound up marrying a Catholic German—talk about ironic!

My grandparents believed immigrants were the people who did menial jobs. Italian men were construction workers, and women were cleaners. Do you see how this kind of stereotyping brainwashes people?

In my quest for freedom from a dysfunctional family life, I moved away from home at a young age. My circle of friends became multicultural, and I began to enjoy life. Quite possibly it was my fantasy of romantic love from the movies I watched, or the trip to Italy I had taken, or maybe even the bonding of the family unit, but my closest friends were mostly Italian. Perhaps I had stereotyped Jewish guys myself, or maybe I just wanted to run far away from my own religion, but mostly I wanted fun relationships with people who knew how to be happy, humble, and unpretentious.

I didn't like dating Jewish guys. I had gone on very few dates before moving away from home to appease my family. I think the stigma of Jewish people having money was prominent while I was growing up, and it must have affected these boys' psyches, because the fellows I dated failed to captivate my interest, especially when bragging about their possessions and accomplishments and successes.

I didn't like that everything in my life was valued based on money. Call me crazy, but I was starved for compassion, heartfelt conversations, and stories about fascinating things about other parts of the world. My two best friends back then, and still today, are Italian and Yugoslavian. Perhaps I just grew up against the grain, but I've lived a wealth of experience and certainly have no regrets.

In demonstrating how certain norms are instilled in us, using my life as an example, I see how we can become products of our environments—but we don't have to remain products. We all have the ability to be in charge of our own lives. Once we set out into the world, we can re-evaluate our upbringings, explore new people and the world, and find where it is we feel comfortable and happy. Don't be fooled: Mother has a propensity to hover in our lives even though we take a new path and adapt to our own newer views on life. We begin to broaden our horizons while the previous generations stay stagnant in their beliefs if they choose not to grow and remain living in their sheltered perceptions. This is where a lot of emotional conflict can arise.

Many women have issues with and from their mothers. Some mothers really do have good intentions with their meddling, and some like to preach their morals, thinking they're only trying to protect us. Some mothers' advice can be destructive to our self-esteem whether they recognize it or not. In many cases, our mothers have suffered hardships in their own lives, which keep them bitter and lashing out at us for their own mistakes or quite possibly out of jealousy for something they weren't able to become. If we don't stand strong in our own beliefs, our egos are susceptible to the things we're told by our mothers.

I have a friend, Sara, who's beautiful and sexy and who exudes self-confidence in her style and personality, yet she's almost fifty and still single. She has plenty of suitors, but they never seem to make the cut. She asked me why I think she never seems to meet the right guy, but it wasn't until later in our friendship that she divulged to me just how dominant of a force her mother is in her life.

Sara's mother is devout to her religion and her old-school beliefs. She experienced something unpleasant when she was younger in her own relationships, and she calls Sara often and berates her about her lifestyle. Sara's a hardworking girl who makes a good living and doesn't have a lot of free time. She's happy with herself and her accomplishments. She takes care of herself and has a great circle of friends. I think her independence and exotic looks are often intimidating to men, but that doesn't stop them from being initially attracted to her. So what's Sara's problem in the relationship department? Her mother.

Words weigh heavy. Sara's mother urges her to stop dressing so fancy, reminding her she's not a young girl anymore. Well, Sara hasn't given up her flair for style, but why do her mother's words cling to her enough that she sabotages her own relationships? Sara's mom constantly meddles in her life, repeating the same comments and directives in every conversation she has with her daughter.

After so much time, those words can brainwash. Sara's mother tells her that men only want her for her looks and her income. Sara gets no uplifting from her mother about her accomplishments and self-worth, and she's never told that any man would be lucky to have her. Instead, she's urged to stay on her own because men are only looking for material things from her. Whenever Sara does meet an eligible partner, she self-sabotages because she's sure the man is only out for one or two things from her. Those thoughts are deeply implanted in Sara's mind from years of being told them by her mother.

Looking in from the outside, I can see this is sheer nonsense. Sara's situation is no different from when I was made to feel inadequate, told I wasn't pretty enough or good enough to succeed. Carrying those thoughts with us hinders our capability to believe in ourselves. One would have to be quite resilient to overcome those negative teachings.

Some mothers try to direct us toward things they may have wanted to be themselves. Some may have good intentions, others may not, but either way, a mother shouldn't be dictating how her children should live their lives based on her perception of life. In other circumstances, maybe we've been chided for who we are or what we choose to do with our lives because our mothers are unsatisfied with how their own lives have turned out. In many cases, a mother may find it difficult to be happy for anyone's accomplishments, even her own children's. This may seem a bit harsh or unbelievable, but it happens. I know it happens because I lived it.

The bottom line is that we are not our mothers. We're our own individual, unique selves. We form our own thoughts and opinions, and we should live our lives the way we see fit. We're not obligated to live out anyone else's dreams. We shouldn't have to appease anyone by doing things we feel are against what we believe in. However, we won't adapt to these lessons overnight, and I'm not saying it's always easy to stand our ground.

There will undoubtedly be hurt feelings when we defy what we're told by family. Change begins with baby steps. At first, we must assess who we want to be and realize our values. When we feel good about ourselves and are comfortable with the decisions we make, and by becoming brave enough to abide by them, we can clear our own paths.

It would be great if we could make all these adjustments and gain the respect and compliance of those who feed us negative comments in our lives, but sometimes, as in my own situation, we're forced to make a decision to walk away for our own good. I'm not advocating severing ties here, merely explaining that in some relationships, we reach a wall that cannot be broken. It's always worth trying to break down that wall, but if it cannot be dismantled without taking our own self-esteem with it, it can be very freeing to walk away and find our happiness instead of living in someone else's misery.

Conquering Fears

From where do our fears originate? I often bat this thought around in my head when I find myself feeling afraid of something or someone. Some of us have a fear of the unknown, and many fears stem from incidents in our lives. I've found myself afraid of many things throughout my life. We don't often consider the origin of our fears, and they tend to create a ripple effect in our lives, hindering us from being who we wish to be.

The mere act of being told as a child that you aren't good enough at something you enjoy doing can have long-term repercussions. Those words remain in our memories and make us feel as though we aren't good enough to excel at the things we want to do. Upon setting out to try a new hobby or profession, we can easily hold ourselves back with negative thoughts of the past. They lurk in our heads, telling us not to bother trying because we already know we aren't good enough to succeed. The baggage we carry from personal criticisms of the past has the propensity to weigh us down with thoughts of inadequacy, crippling our enthusiasm for our desires.

I spent most of my life afraid of my own mother, but as I got older, I wanted to find out what made me so afraid of her, which then led me to question why I was afraid of so many other things. I wanted to find answers for my shortcomings, and I had never really given much thought to why I had so many fears. Certain things just terrified me, and I wanted to discover why and find resolution.

If we go back into our pasts, we can usually relate our fears back to their catalysts. For example, I am afraid of the dark. I have been all my life. In fact, when I was a child, I wouldn't go to sleep unless the bedroom light was left on. A lamp wouldn't suffice; it had to be the ceiling light. Many kids are afraid of the dark. Seeds are planted by the activities we engage in, and our overactive imaginations can stimulate thoughts about all the scary things that can happen in the dark.

When I was a child, I loved to watch scary movies and play with an Ouija board. Those movies preyed on me when it was dark. I particularly remember the movie *Psycho*. Heck, I couldn't take a shower for the rest of my teen years without having my little brother stand outside the bathroom door until I got out for fear that Norman Bates was behind the curtain. Those kinds of movies scared the hell out of me long after I watched them.

I also had a curiosity about the occult and encountered some eerie times while trying to sleep, knowing that an ominous Ouija board was stacked on the cupboard shelf five feet from my bed. These types of fears followed me through life. Sure, when I got older, I realized that there was no such thing as the boogeyman, but I couldn't shake the fears I had kept with me since childhood.

When I moved away from home, into my own apartment, I had to learn how to deal with my fear of the dark. It didn't just vanish, so I had to find a way to live with it in order to function in daily life. I established a ritual, which helped me feel more comfortable with my fear every time I came home at night to my empty apartment. I walked inside and opened all the closet doors to make sure nobody was inside. I always looked behind the shower curtain and, yes, under the bed. Was I obsessive? Yes, I was, but once I deemed the coast clear, my mind was at ease and I felt safe, able to sleep at night without wondering whether someone was waiting to jump out of the closet and kill me.

It isn't hard to realize how much our fears can dominate our thoughts. Fear in any aspect of our lives has to be dealt with in a manner that allows us to feel comfortable in our own skin. If I hadn't found a way to deal with my fear, I may well have wound up living like a hermit. As much as my fears were very real to me, I had to figure out a way to confront them so they wouldn't hamper my lifestyle.

I also have a huge fear of dogs. I've had it all my life and can't even figure out why. I've never really given much thought to why I'm afraid, but I've been asked hundreds of times. I don't have any concrete answers, but a distant memory of being chased for blocks by an angry German Shepherd I outran when I was seven looms in my memory. Friends with dogs try to pacify me, assuring me that their dogs won't bite, yet this is something I just can't get past. I can't be comfortable with a dog around me, large or small.

I know we can't dodge all the things we fear in life, but I still had to find a way to work around this one. I usually just choose not to go to someone's home if I know they have a dog. I don't like to put anyone out by asking them to lock up a pet who's like a child to them. Those friends come to visit me instead.

The point is that all types of fears can hinder us from doing things we enjoy, but if we can't learn to overcome those fears, we at least need to find a way to cope so we don't become shrinking violets. We may also be afraid to voice our opinions in remembrance of a reprimanding from the past, but we shouldn't be. As long as we aren't trash talking someone, we have the right to express ourselves. What's the worst that can happen? Someone may not agree with you, but nobody's opinions are ever going to satisfy everyone, and we shouldn't have to go through life hiding who we are.

I've often encountered women who were afraid to wear certain styles of clothing. Many women self-criticize, wishing they could wear a certain style but not daring to because they may be slightly overweight, or perhaps they think they'll be laughed at or perceived differently by their peers or family. Why should they hold back from wearing something they feel expresses their taste and style? Most of the time, self-doubt is instilled by a past experience or by a controlling force in one's life who dictates how she should dress. That doesn't mean the criticizer is correct, only that she has shallow opinions or may herself be insecure.

It's human nature for us to allow negative responses to our personal choices to hinder our confidence levels if we're insecure in our own skin. However, a jealous person forbidding his or her spouse to dress in a certain manner is usually suffering from his or her own issues with jealousy.

If we don't take responsibility for our own choices, we can become ruled by someone else's power. This results in us giving up pieces of our own identities to satisfy the whims of someone else, leaving us with little self-esteem. We begin to say things such as "I can't wear that. I'm too heavy" or "My spouse wouldn't let me out of the house in this." The first statement reflects a low opinion of oneself. The latter reflects that someone is allowing him or herself to be governed by others. Neither is helpful to self-esteem.

Clothing comes in all different sizes, so everyone has a personal choice. Everyone has the ability to project him or herself as beautiful and confident. Be daring! Step out of your comfort zones and put on something that personifies you and makes you feel happy. The trick is to wear your confidence—not just your clothing. Stand proud when you walk. Put on a little blush, mascara, and lipstick, and, most of all, put on a smile. You'll be surprised to find how openly others will receive you. It's easy enough to put on a nice outfit and wear a sour face with it. You may attract an instant glance at your beautiful outfit, but as soon as your persona is taken for miserable, nobody is going to want to hang around. Why do you think there are many beautiful, sexy single women? Aside from a personal choice to be single, their packaging may only be able to last so long before it has to be opened up. If that physically beautiful woman has no goodness, humor, or happiness to share, people won't want to stick around for the long haul.

Listen, nobody says it's going to be easy to overhaul our dispositions in life, and this will be a work in progress for those of us who've spent too many years self-criticizing and being influenced by what others have told us to do. If we begin with small steps, time will eventually provide us with more confidence as we continue to make positive changes. We need to go beyond our comfort levels and try new things.

Try taking yourself to a clothing store without a naysayer, either alone or with a positive friend, for a second opinion on the outfits you try on. Treat yourself to a new pair of shoes and a lipstick. Then look in the mirror and gauge your happiness. Focus on your beautiful bits and notice how much more positively people perceive and receive you. Don't beat yourself up if certain clothes don't look so great—move on to the next ones. Not everything looks good on everyone, no matter how slim they may be. Find yourself clothes that accentuate your finer features, and stop focusing on the negative. Be fearless and know that nobody is perfect. Everyone has something beautiful to offer.

Exposing our Personality Through the Internet

Many people assume they can hide themselves or pretend to be somebody else on the Internet. For a myriad of reasons, people will use a different persona or alter ego in the cyber world. It's easy to hide ourselves on the web, but depending on our goals, situations can become sticky when we use facades. No matter our motives for lying, we have to consider how far that deceit can really take us.

Let's take Internet dating, for example. Many people bloat their bios, putting up old pictures of themselves, taken at a time when they liked themselves better, or even putting up entirely fake pictures. These tactics are used in the hopes of snagging a potential suitor, and this happens a lot, but if one is looking for sincerity in a relationship and hoping to form a bond, the charade will only last until it's time to actually meet the other person. Then what happens?

We can't hide forever, so why not be honest and seek the truth by finding out whether that suitor is really interested in who we are? After all, the gig is up when we actually meet our interested party, so starting out with honesty makes the process so much easier, saving us from pretending and having to keep track of the lies we tell along the way. Don't we want people to like and love us for who we really are?

The whole identity issue goes back to being able to love ourselves. People who don't love themselves feel they have to pretend to be somebody else. We need to accentuate our positives, acknowledging our strengths, desires, and accomplishments to ourselves first before we can ask others to believe in us. We need to feel worthy that we have something to offer, whether from the heart or the mind.

We all have the ability to seek the goodness within ourselves. We can talk about things we know about, books we've read, and places we've been to or one day hope to visit. By talking, we express who we are and what we care about, what interests us. This is all part of personality and character. Maybe our passion is for our children, our hobbies, or a cause we believe in. All these things show heart and compassion. By keeping true to our authentic selves and sharing our enthusiasm with others, although our passions may not appeal to everyone, we will eventually connect with someone who appreciates our attributes.

By sharing our thoughts, we emit character. Not all of this will happen overnight, but if we take this advice in stride and adapt it to our lives, we will attract likeminded people. This applies to dating profiles, blogs, and casual conversation.

Did you know you can actually feel someone smiling through his or her words? It's true. Smiles aren't only visual. You can sense them when you're reading a book or an article the same way you can sense them in a chat box or personal bio. When somebody reads your bio, he or she receives an evaluation of who you are.

Words are powerful, so use them wisely and to their best potential. Everything you say and write on the Internet follows you. Being cohesive with your words and actions makes conversations effortless because you won't have to second guess everything you say to keep up with your falsehoods. It can become quite burdensome, living in lies. Celebrate who you are, and be that person.

When I began my public journey on the Internet, the first thing I had to come to terms with baring my raw self to the world. As a nonfiction author who writes about life experiences, it took me a lot of time before I felt comfortable sharing my journey publicly. I wanted to build a following with my readers, but I was uncomfortable with exposing my personal self. I certainly couldn't pretend to be someone I wasn't, given my public image and the genre I write in, so I wasn't about to create an image of myself that didn't correlate with what my writing represented.

I found myself quite overwhelmed, but with time, I created my blog and website and joined the world of social media. Through sharing my views and opinions on writing and publishing, and the true events of my life, I attracted readers who could identify with what I had to say. I was still me, only now I was sharing my world publicly instead of privately.

My writing certainly doesn't resonate with everyone, but those who enjoy reading nonfiction stories about life that they can identify with and take a message from are the people I attract. I write with my authentic voice, no differently than how I would speak to someone in the real world. My voice doesn't change from my blogging to my book writing, because it's who I am. I'm not a fictional character in a book, nor am I an Internet imposter. I am myself. My sincerity and humor don't change just because I'm talking to someone through emails, chats, or messages. It would be dishonest of me to mislead anyone about my true persona.

I didn't have to make up a personality, so I can always be the same person to everyone I meet. My author picture is beside all social media where my name appears, identifying me, so I can't hide. I used to be surprised when I got nice comments about my wit or humor. How could someone get all that from something I wrote? I realized my personality came through in my writing—and all of you have no doubt formed some sort of impression of me by now!

All the things I've talked about revolve around being our authentic selves. We shouldn't have to be chameleons, adjusting our personalities to fit others' interests. If we can just be ourselves, eventually those who share the same interests and values will gravitate toward us.

Forming Healthier Relationships

When forming friendships and relationships of the heart, we tend to gravitate toward likeminded individuals, or we attract people based on how we represent ourselves. People with healthy attitudes about themselves tend to fall into relationships with those who share similar attitudes and values. The level of self-confidence we project sets the tone for who we attract.

Women will often ask, "How did that girl latch on to him? What did he see in her?" Do you ever look at a couple and notice that perhaps one of them isn't particularly attractive while the other is? You're left scratching your head, trying to figure out what the attraction was, without realizing there's so much more to our composition than physical appeal. More than likely, kindness, wittiness, and compassion sparked those relationships. The traits we expose of our personalities are what calls attention to us.

People like to be around happy, positive people. Those qualities are natural attracters. Physical beauty and sexiness aren't enough to solidify a relationship if someone has nothing more to offer. Yes, it's true that there are some shallow people out there who'll only go out with "beautiful" people, but if those people continue relationships based only on looks, they may find their partners displaying other negative qualities—and at that point they have sacrificed happiness for vanity. It does happen. Physical beauty alone is no foundation for a happy, healthy relationship.

Sometimes, other couples' relationships may seem ideal when we're looking from the outside in, but we don't know what goes on behind closed doors. We may lament, "Why can't I get a guy like that?" But would we really want to be involved with someone if we found out he or she was incompatible with our standards and values? I wouldn't.

Many women tend to fall into a pattern of repeatedly attracting the same type of "wrong" guy. Why is that? Let's think about it for a moment. More often than not, how we project ourselves determines the type of people we attract. I've seen it happen to friends of mine. When asked, I try to tell them what I see in their patterns with relationships, but just because they've asked, that doesn't necessarily mean they want to change their patterns.

Much of who we attract stems from our way of thinking. If people don't value themselves highly and continue to be self-critical or perhaps too allowing of indiscretions, they leave themselves open to attracting people who can detect those vulnerabilities. Many men are attracted to these types of women because being with a woman with weak self-esteem makes them feel more powerful or superior. By winning over a woman's affections and boosting her ego with attention and compliments, which he knows she so desperately needs to feel better about herself, such a man can come off as a hero despite his shortcomings.

These women, with low self-esteem, thrive on the idea that someone else would even want to be involved with them. This leaves these women vulnerable and exposed to whatever a man says or does.

Other women may be drawn to the "bad boy" type. This is the kind of guy women know instinctively is not good for them, yet they find his edge stimulating and exciting. More often than not, strong and secure women are unhappy in these relationships because of the calculating tactics and persuasiveness used by the man.

Keep in mind that negative, depressing attitudes are going to attract people with those same qualities—and sometimes nobody at all. In the same light, if one finds a companion with whom he or she can complain and bitch, neither of them will grow into positive human beings regardless of how much they enjoy one another's company. These types of people most likely won't have a circle of friends interested in sharing their lives.

They say opposites attract. Surely they can, because variety can be very stimulating to a relationship. With that said, "opposites" can mean different things. Opposite attractions can mean different tastes, preferences, and opinions, but in a good working relationship, although each partner retains his or her own individual preferences, both partners' morals and values in life are matched. For those who don't share similar values, the attraction is merely that—an attraction to the opposite.

We shouldn't self-criticize, wishing we were more attractive, slim, or intelligent. Developing a healthy self-esteem is about loving ourselves for everything we already are. We should be embracing our God-given gifts and using them to their highest potentials. Good hygiene, a neat and aesthetically pleasing appearance, and a smile all convey a good disposition. Keeping our troubles to ourselves or saving them for conversations with friends is a good policy when meeting new people, as the general population isn't really eager to talk to people who dump their troubles and negative attitudes about life on others upon first meeting. That's just the way the universe works.

I like to put myself in others' shoes when comparing situations. If I met someone and began speaking about all my ailments, talking negatively about certain issues or even singing my own praises, I'm willing to wager the person would say, "Nice meeting you" and find an excuse to move on. I know I would politely do the same. We all have crap in our lives, but such conversations are by no means attention grabbers.

Personally, I prefer to spread joy wherever I go. I have a tendency to make friends easily. I don't attribute this to anything more than my persona. Any time I go out, anywhere, even grocery shopping, I always try to look my best. My clothes are neat and clean, my hair is styled, and I put on some makeup, if only lipstick and mascara. This is the way I've maintained my own standards on the road to loving myself. Being well dressed and attractive doesn't necessarily denote that someone is a friendly person, but gestures and kind words do. Those traits reveal our personalities.

I'm the type of person who talks to everyone. It doesn't matter whether I'm in a store, at an airport, or picking up my mail. I always say hi and ask how people are doing, and I always wear a smile. This invites good rapport with people. It's not about making friends with the whole world but more about leaving nice footprints behind. You never know—every so often, we may just click with someone in our travels, and a special friendship may develop.

You don't have to be a writer to project what you believe. Whoever you are and whatever you do, it's always best (and so much easier) to stay authentic to who you are. It's really a very small world, and you never know when and where you will meet up with people again.

Epilogue

Many of us have been scathed by emotional wounds in our pasts. Whether we've realized these slights or habitually taken them as a natural part of life, they were indeed injustices to our self-esteem.

Subconsciously, the remnants of many of our inflicted hurts remain engraved in our psyches and play an integral role in our confidence levels. Recognizing and confronting our prior hurts is a strong beginning to rectifying those feelings. Taking positive actions to overcome our emotional wounds is the first step in altering our perception, stepping away from the belief that all the negativity we were given was true. It wasn't!

Take ownership of yourself and your feelings. We cannot subject ourselves to negative people or environments. Evaluate yourself and all the things you've overcome in life, and celebrate yourself by keeping a positive attitude and focusing on your best assets instead of dragging yourself down and self-criticizing. Look for ways to better yourself and emphasize all the good attributes you do possess.

Remember that negativity breeds more negativity. There's no value in it. Dwelling on things that make us unhappy only leads to more unhappiness. By opening our minds and focusing on the positive, we allow more positive experiences to come our way. This is the law of attraction. It's a cycle, and it's a fact that if we focus our thoughts on negative things, it becomes difficult to see the good in anything.

This is all a process to train our minds. It's a gradual learning curve. We all know it takes time to adapt to adjustments. Consider the process like taking a course in school. Change may be difficult in the beginning because it's new to us, but by the end of the semester, we have the potential to become A students. Life is a course. We need only master it as we do anything else to graduate and accomplish our goal of mending our self-esteem. Nothing is as freeing as breaking the chains that bind our spirits.

I wish you peace and success. Remember to love thyself first.

End

About the Author

D.G. Kaye was born and resides in Toronto, Canada. Kaye is a nonfiction writer of memoirs about her life experiences, matters of the heart, and women's issues. She is the author of *Conflicted Hearts* and *Meno-What? A Memoir*.

Kaye began writing when pen and paper became tools to express her pent-up emotions during a turbulent childhood. Kaye's writing began as notes and cards she wrote for the people she loved and admired when she was afraid to use her voice. Through the years, Kaye journaled about her life, writing about her opinions on people and events. She later began writing poetry and health articles for a Canadian magazine when her interest was piqued by natural healthcare. She began writing books a few years ago to share her stories and inspiration.

When she isn't writing, Kaye loves to read, shop, travel, and play poker. Her favorite genres of reading are biographies, memoirs, health, and writing.

Kaye believes in paying it forward. She says, "For every kindness, there should be kindness in return. Wouldn't that just make the world right?"

Visit Kaye's website and blog at www.dgkayewriter.com.
Follow on Twitter: www.twitter.com/pokercubster
Follow on Google: www.google.com/+DebbyDGKayeGies
Follow on Facebook: www.facebook.com/dgkaye
Follow on LinkedIn: www.linkedin.com/in/dgkaye7

Check out D.G.'s books:

Conflicted Hearts
www.conflictedhearts.com
www.smarturl.it/bookconflictedhearts

Meno-What? A Memoir
www.menowhatthememoir.com
www.smarturl.it/MenoWhatAMemoir

Read an excerpt from the book!
Read more about D.G. at www.amazon.com/author/dgkaye7.

If you'd like to contact D.G. Kaye or sign up for updates on her next books, email her at d.g.kaye.writer@gmail.com and join her mailing list at her website, www.dgkayewriter.com.

www.ingramcontent.com/pod-product-compliance
Lightning Source LLC
LaVergne TN
LVHW041226080426
835508LV00011B/1091